The ABCs of Avalanche Safety

Sue A. Ferguson
Edward R. LaChapelle

THIRD EDITION

THE MOUNTAINEERS BOOKS

Published by
The Mountaineers Books
1001 SW Klickitat Way, Suite 201
Seattle, WA 98134

© 2003 by Sue A. Ferguson and Edward R. LaChapelle

First edition 1961; reissued 1978. Second edition 1985. Third edition 2003.

Published simultaneously in Great Britain by Cordee, 3a DeMontfort Street, Leicester, England, LE1 7HD

Manufactured in Canada

Project Editor: Christine Ummel Hosler
Editor: Julie Van Pelt
Cover and book design: The Mountaineers Books
Layout artist: Kristy Welch, Peggy Egerdahl
Illustrator: Jennifer LaRock Shontz, Red Shoe Design
Cover photograph: *Skier outrunning avalanche* © Lee Cohen/Corbis
Frontispiece: *Powder avalanche*

Library of Congress Cataloging-in-Publication Data
Ferguson, Sue A.
  The ABCs of avalanche safety.— 3rd ed. / by Sue Ferguson and E.R. LaChapelle.
    p. cm.
Rev. ed. of: ABC of avalanche safety / Edward R. LaChapelle.
Includes bibliographical references and index.
  ISBN 0-89886-885-8 (paperbound)
  1. Avalanches. I. LaChapelle, Edward R. II. LaChapelle, Edward R. ABC of avalanche safety. III. Title.
  QC929.A8F47 2003
  363.34'9—dc21

                                        2003006777

Contents

Explanation of Terms 8

CHAPTER 1
Snow and Avalanche Basics 19
   The Snow Cover 19
   Avalanche Characteristics 31
   Terrain 41

CHAPTER 2
Practical Guidelines for Stability Evaluation 44
   The Evidence about Snow Stability 44
   Analyzing the Evidence 61
   Specific Situations 65

CHAPTER 3
Safety Rules and Rescue 73
   Minimizing Avalanche Risks 73
   Rescue by Survivors 81
   Organized Rescue Actions 93
   Technical Aids to Locating a Victim 103

CHAPTER 4

Case Histories

Case Histories 112

Spring Ski Tour to Paradise Valley,
Mount Rainier, April 1976 113
Training Course in the Cariboo Mountains
of British Columbia, January 1976 115
Avalanches in Banff National Park, March 1977 .. 119
Six Events in the Cascade Mountains 121
A Week of Ski Touring on the Ruth Glacier
(Mount McKinley), April 1983 123
Summary 126

Appendix A
Avalanche Rescue Caches 128

Appendix B
Avalanche Accident and Rescue Report 131

Appendix C
Avalanche Information Bulletins 133

Short Bibliography of Avalanche Literature 136
Index 139

A NOTE ABOUT SAFETY

Safety is an important concern in all outdoor activities. No book can alert you to every hazard or anticipate the limitations of every reader. The descriptions of techniques and procedures in this book are intended to provide general information. This is not a complete text on avalanche science. Nothing substitutes for formal instruction, routine practice, and plenty of experience. When you follow any of the procedures described here, you assume responsibility for your own safety. Use this book as a general guide to further information. Under normal conditions, excursions into the backcountry require attention to traffic, road and trail conditions, weather, terrain, the capabilities of your party, and other factors. Keeping informed on current conditions and exercising common sense are the keys to a safe, enjoyable outing.

The Mountaineers Books

Explanation of Terms

An *avalanche* is a large mass in motion down a mountainside or over a precipice. According to Webster, an avalanche may consist of snow, rock, earth, or mud. In practice, however, the term is reserved in English-speaking countries almost exclusively for the snow avalanche. Other types require additional description, such as "avalanche of rock." The more general term commonly used in the United States is *slide*, which may mean any of the substances mentioned above, unless specifically qualified, as in *snowslide.* The term *slide* is taken to mean "snowslide" only when used in a context where the meaning is unequivocal. *Snowslide* and *avalanche* may be used interchangeably to describe the same phenomenon, the difference being only in their respective Anglo-Saxon and French roots. Sometimes, uninformed users of the terms introduce their own distinctions, as in the case of a motorist on a mountain pass who found the highway blocked by an avalanche. When asked why he had ignored broadcast warnings, he replied, "I heard on the radio there was danger of snowslides. If I had known you were going to have avalanches, I wouldn't have come."

Figure 1. The release zone, track, and deposition zone of a typical avalanche path.

An avalanche can fall only where snow has collected on an inclined surface, usually a mountainside. Among avalanche workers this layer of snow often is referred to as the *snow cover,* a direct translation from the German "Schneedecke." German is the language in which much of the widely used avalanche terminology originated, owing to early Swiss leadership in this field. In the United States, hydrologists like to call the same layer of snow the *snowpack.* The two terms are synonymous.

Avalanches normally recur from time to time in the same mountain locality, called the *avalanche path.* The mean length of time between occurrences is the *return interval.* This path consists of three parts. The *release zone* is the area at the top of the path where the avalanche starts; it usually involves the breakaway zone for slab avalanches (see below) and is characterized by accelerating motion. The *track* is the middle part of the path, where steady-state velocity usually prevails unless modified by local terrain variations. There is little or no deposition of avalanched snow in the track. Below the track is the *runout zone* (sometimes called the *deposition zone*); usually less steep than the release zone and track, this is the zone in which avalanche motion decelerates and deposition takes place. (See Figure 1.) These distinctions of path parts are of more than academic interest. A prime rule for safe travel in avalanche terrain is STAY OUT OF THE RELEASE ZONES; hence, it pays to make the physical as well as the linguistic distinction.

Avalanches come in all sizes, ranging from very small ones, called *sluffs* (a spelling corruption of "sloughs"), which

Figure 2. Loose-snow (point release) avalanche. ▶

by definition do not run more than 50 meters, to very large ones involving millions of tons of snow capable of devastating whole mountainsides. In casual usage the latter kind are sometimes called *climax avalanches,* although scientific workers are careful to reserve the term for avalanches of any size that result from a sequence of meteorological causes rather than from a single snowstorm. The two usages for "climax" may apply to the same avalanche, but not necessarily. Avalanches in which only the top layers of snow break loose and slide on an underlying snow surface are *surface avalanches.* Those involving the entire snow cover sliding on the ground are *full-depth avalanches.* Avalanches on open slopes are *unconfined avalanches.* Those whose tracks lie partly or entirely in gullies or ravines are *channeled.*

Two basic types of avalanches are recognized according to conditions prevailing at the point of origin. The *loose-snow avalanche* originates at a point and propagates downhill by dislodging successively larger amounts of poorly cohering snow grains, typically gaining in width as it falls (Figure 2). The behavior of avalanching loose snow is analogous to that of dry sand. On the other hand, when cohesion among snow grains increases, large areas of the release zone may break away all at once in the form of a *slab avalanche.* A distinct, cohesive layer of the snow cover then slides on a clearly defined *gliding surface,* often facilitated by the presence of a weak or cohesionless snow layer called the *lubricating layer.* The division between the sliding slab and the

Figure 3. The crown, flank, and stauchwall of a typical slab avalanche. ▶

stable snow above and to the sides is called the *fracture line*. These terms for slab avalanche features are direct translations from German equivalents.

A different nomenclature, which follows long-standing usage for analogous features in soil mechanics, has become more common. In this usage the gliding surface is called the *bed surface;* the top fracture line, the *crown surface;* and the side fracture lines, the *flank surfaces*. The lubricating layer is called a *weak layer* or *weak interface*. In both terminologies, the surface of compression failure at the downhill edge of the slab forms a shallow berm, the *stauchwall,* a German label, which apparently has no equivalent in English-language soil mechanics. The stauchwall marks the upper edge of snows overridden by the falling slab. (See Figure 3.) Slab avalanches are distinguished as *hard* or *soft* according to whether the slab snow has enough cohesion to remain in lumps as it falls or whether it breaks up into a mass of loose snow. While the exact terminology may vary, the physical distinction of different avalanche types is of great practical importance. Most large avalanches and most of those involving accidents (whether large or small) are slab avalanches. The reason a mountain traveler is exhorted to stay out of the release zones is because disturbance of the snow there may provide the *trigger* to initiate fracturing of a slab.

Avalanches are further classified as *wet* or *dry* according to whether or not liquid water is present in the snow at the point of origin. Knowledge on this point may be uncertain. On the other hand, avalanche debris deposited in the

Figure 4. A wet-snow avalanche. ▶

runout zone has a distinctly different character according to whether or not liquid water is present in the snow—and the difference is easily recognized. Because of high water content in wet snow, there is higher friction at the sliding surface than with flowing dry snow. This causes wet-snow avalanches to travel more slowly than dry-snow avalanches, and wet avalanches follow terrain features as they descend more easily than dry avalanches. In addition, wet avalanches often create scoring marks in the sliding surface

Figure 5. A powder avalanche.

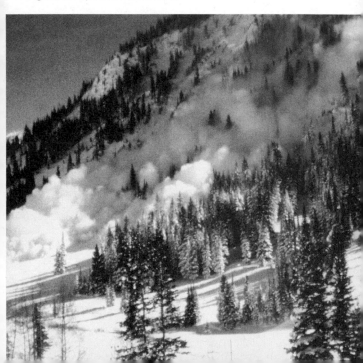

and entrain rocks, dirt, and other material. When avalanches fall over long paths, however, they sometimes originate in dry snow but experience sufficient melt in descent that they form deposits as wet snow.

An exceptionally wet avalanche is called a *slush flow*. Slush flows typically occur on relatively shallow slopes (5° to 25°) with an impermeable bed surface such as rock or permafrost, which allow meltwater to pool at the base of the snowpack. They release by intense snowmelt or heavy rain. They are common in polar and subpolar drainage basins where cold, dry winters promote the development of shallow, coarse-grained snow covers and spring warming can occur suddenly.

Dry snow falling at appreciable velocities conveys some of the snow particles into the air to form a *dust cloud,* much of which travels with *turbulent motion.* If the dust cloud predominates, such avalanches are sometimes called *powder snow avalanches,* or simply *powder avalanches* (Figure 5). If a sufficiently dense aerosol is formed by the snow particles entrained in the air, the dust cloud may behave as an atmospheric turbidity current, rushing ahead of the sliding snow at high velocity and occasionally inflicting heavy damage through *wind blast* or *air blast.* Another theory suggests that air blasts occur when free-falling (airborne) avalanches strike the ground, compressing the air underneath, generating a pressure wave that moves ahead of the debris.

The snow cover on a mountainside is subjected to gravitational forces that cause gradual deformations as well as the sudden fall of avalanches. Compression of the snow perpendicular to the slope under its own weight is called *settlement.* Internal deformation parallel to the slope is *creep*, while displacement of the entire snow cover along the ground surface is *glide*. On an irregular mountainside, or where snow depth varies, or both, these deformations vary in time and space, thereby inducing stresses in the snow cover.

Elastically stored strain energy in the snow may be released to propagate fracturing in the form of a slab avalanche or, if the snow layers remain in place, in the form of *glide cracks*. Under certain conditions favorable to glide, the snow cover may slowly accelerate, widening the cracks and making an increasingly rapid transition to avalanche velocities. Japanese investigators have termed this phenomenon the *transavalanche*, a contraction of the term "transition avalanche."

CHAPTER 1
Snow and Avalanche Basics

THE SNOW COVER

The reader is urged to give careful attention to the following fundamentals before proceeding to the practical aspects of hazard evaluation. Though a purely empirical knowledge of snow can serve in many instances, a thorough understanding of the basic physical processes involved is essential to interpret observations intelligently.

SNOW CRYSTAL FORMATION

When atmospheric conditions favor condensation of water vapor at temperatures below freezing, various types of snow crystals form (Figure 6). Resultant shapes are a function of temperature and available moisture (water vapor). *Needle* and *sheath* shapes form when the atmosphere is warm. Cold atmospheres with low moisture content favor *column* shapes. As moisture content increases in a cold atmosphere, *plates* become more common, then *dendrites* (stellar crystals). When liquid water droplets exist in the atmosphere at

below-freezing temperatures (super cooled) they can freeze onto precipitating crystals or other surfaces, forming a layer of rime. Heavy riming hides the shape of the original crystal, forming a particle called *graupel* or *soft hail*. If graupel is then melted and refrozen, as is common in thunderclouds, it becomes a hard, icy form of hail. Sleet is a frozen raindrop. In addition to formation in the atmosphere, crystals can form directly onto the snow surface as frost. The needle or feather shapes are called *hoarfrost* or commonly *surface hoar*.

Density of newly fallen snow often depends on air temperature as well as crystal type. The lightest snow falls under cold, calm conditions. The highest densities are associated with graupel, needle crystals, and crystals broken by wind that fell at temperatures near freezing.

FORMATION OF THE SNOW COVER

The snow cover accumulates layer by layer with a resulting stratification that displays the history of the weather variations that occurred during its buildup. With the passage of time, structural and crystalline changes within the snow cover (metamorphism) obscure the original stratification and convert the snow into new forms. The layered structure of the snow is a key factor in avalanche formation. The layers have different strengths, and the bond between two adjacent layers can vary widely. When this bond is weak, the layer above it can slide off the one below—the

◀ *Figure 6. Snow crystal forms: A) plate, B) stellar or dendrite, C) column, D) needle and sheath with some rime modules, E) capped column, F) graupel, and G) surface hoar.*

basic criterion for slab avalanches. Metamorphic changes alter layer and bond strengths with time. These changes may either increase or decrease snow stability, depending on prevailing temperature conditions.

Metamorphism within the snow cover is a continuous process that begins when the snow is deposited and continues until it melts. The most common type of snow metamorphism reshapes crystals into rounded grains that eventually bond together into simple chains. Because the resulting rounded shapes are relatively stable forms of ice, the process is called *equilibrium metamorphism* (Figure 7). Some refer to equilibrium metamorphism as *radius-dependent recrystallization* because water vapor is transferred by sublimation from sharp peaks and ridges of a crystal (which have small, convex radii of curvature) to hollows and valleys (which have concave radii of curvature). The radius dependency also allows crystals to bond together in the valley-shaped places where they touch, forming relatively strong chains of grains. As it tends to destroy the original shape of a feathery crystal, this process formerly was called *destructive metamorphism*. Also, it has been called *equi-temperature metamorphism* (ET) because external forces, such as gradients in temperature, are thought to be negligible. Strongly influenced by ambient temperature, the process proceeds rapidly near the freezing point. At extremely low temperatures metamorphism is very slow, and it practically stops

Figure 7. Equilibrium metamorphism: A) sharp crystal edges begin to round, B) original crystal shapes become unrecognizable, C) rounded grains form bonded chains.

below -40°C. Because this process takes place with all types of snow crystals, they all tend to approach the uniform condition of rounded grains. The rate of metamorphism is influenced by pressure as well as temperature, with the weight of additional snowfalls accelerating metamorphism of the layer beneath.

Kinetic-growth metamorphism (formerly called *temperature-gradient [TG]* or *constructive metamorphism*) also may take place in the snow cover (Figure 8). This occurs when ice is transferred from one part of the snow cover to another by water vapor diffusion along temperature gradients. The deposition of this vapor around new centers of crystallization forms ice crystals with quite a different character from those of the original snow. These new crystals tend to develop facets or a square shape at first and then assume a scroll or cup shape, appear to be layered, and often grow to several millimeters in diameter. During kinetic growth, forces caused by differences in radius of curvature are negligible. Therefore, very little bonding between crystals occurs. The resulting snow—known as *depth hoar* or, popularly, *sugar snow*—is very fragile, losing all cohesion upon collapse and becoming very soft when wet. The conditions required for its formation are a rapid change of temperature with depth (steep temperature gradient), which causes diffusion of water vapor within the snow cover, and air permeability sufficiently high to permit diffusion to take place. These

◀ *Figure 8. Kinetic-growth metamorphism: A) facets begin forming on crystal edges, B) striations become visible, C) cup and scroll shapes emerge.*

A
```
0        0.5        1
      Millimeters
```

B
```
0        0.5        1
      Millimeters
```

C
```
0         1         2
      Millimeters
```

conditions are most common in early winter, when the snow cover is shallow and unconsolidated.

Kinetic-growth snow plays a very important role in avalanche formation. It is responsible for much of the weakness of snow layers and, sometimes, of layer bonds. It is not necessary for complete crystals of depth hoar to form for the snow to become unstable. Even a partial recrystallization may reduce snow strength enough to cause failure under additional load from new snowfalls or wind drift. As kinetic growth advances, the snow not only loses strength but becomes stiffer (viscosity increases). This is also important for avalanche formation, because stiffer snow is less able to relieve stresses by internal deformation, allowing for sudden, massive collapses once the build-up of stresses finally causes failure.

The presence of liquid water around snow crystals causes metamorphism to proceed more rapidly than under dry conditions, distinguishing *wet metamorphism* (Figure 9) from other processes. While radius-dependent forces dominate wet metamorphism, rounding occurs so quickly that size differences between rounded grains play an important role. Big grains with large radii of curvature continue growing while grains with smaller radii of curvature tend to shrink, resulting in uniform-sized grains that become about a millimeter or so in diameter. Bonding between wet grains occurs in clusters. The clusters of large, round grains remain

◀ *Figure 9. Wet metamorphism: A) large grains grow at the expense of small grains, B) rounded grain shapes dominate, C) wet grains from bonded clusters.*

weak while wet, but form strong crusts of ice when the liquid surrounding the grain clusters freezes.

MECHANICAL PROPERTIES OF THE SNOW COVER

Snow is a plastic material having both elastic and viscous properties. Its viscous nature allows snow to deform internally by creeping and accommodating the motions of gliding (*creep* and *glide* are defined in the Explanation of Terms at the beginning of this book). Both movements are highly dependent on temperature, for snow is least viscous (more easily deformed) near the freezing point, but becomes increasingly stiff (resists deformation) at lower temperatures. Its elastic properties allow snow to store strain energy. Elastic properties become prominent at high rates of loading and strain energy often is released by fracturing. The tensile and shear stresses produced by uneven creep and glide of the snow cover are an important factor in avalanche formation.

Variations in the strength characteristics of snow are among the widest found in nature. The hardness of wind-packed old snow or frozen firn may be as much as 50,000 times that of light, fluffy powder snow. Snow strength continually changes as a result of metamorphism, but also depends on temperature. When snow is disturbed mechanically, then allowed to set, it undergoes a process known as *age hardening*. This process is more pronounced at lower temperatures. The greatest source of mechanical disturbance in nature is the wind, and an increase in hardness is always associated with wind-drifted snow.

THERMAL PROPERTIES OF THE SNOW COVER

Because the mechanical properties of snow are so dependent on temperature, the manner in which heat is lost or gained by the snow cover is important. There are three basic characteristics of snow that strongly influence its thermal properties. First is the high heat of fusion of ice. For each gram of ice existing at the freezing point, approximately 335 Joules (80 calories) are required to convert it to liquid water without any change in temperature. The second is the very low heat conductivity of snow, up to 10,000 times less than that of copper. The third is the presence within the snow cover of water in the form of vapor or liquid, as well as ice. Vapor and liquid water play an important part in heat transfer within the snow cover.

The heat supply at the bottom of the snow pack is relatively limited. A certain amount of heat is stored in the surface layers of earth each summer, and this will melt some of the snow during the winter. If cold weather precedes the first snowfall, however, some of this heat is lost. In any case, an appreciable snow cover insulates the ground surface from external heat exchange. The stored heat is usually sufficient to melt small quantities of snow throughout the winter. The occurrence of melting at the snow–earth interface means that the temperature must stay at the melting point. For this reason the bottom of any appreciable snow cover is almost always at a temperature of 0°C (32° F) throughout the Temperate Zones.

Heat is both lost and gained in much larger quantities at the snow surface, and the temperature undergoes wide fluctuations below the freezing point. The temperature of the snow surface, which is composed of ice (snow grains), can never be higher than 0°C, because ice melts above this point. The principal media of heat transfer at the snow surface are air turbulence, long- and shortwave radiation, condensation-evaporation-sublimation, rainfall, and internal conduction. The medium with the largest potential is air turbulence. Heat may be conveyed to or removed from the snow surface in large quantities by the process known as *eddy conduction,* or the turbulent transfer of heat. This process depends on the motion of air over the snow surface and therefore does not occur in completely still air. The amount of snow that can be melted by a strong, warm wind, such as a Chinook, is much greater than can be melted in a given length of time by any other natural source, including the sun.

Large amounts of energy arrive at the earth's surface in the form of shortwave (visible) radiation from the sun, but up to 90% of the shortwave radiation arriving at the surface of fresh snow is turned back by reflection. In contrast, snow both absorbs and radiates longwave (infrared) radiation freely. In fact, among all substances in nature, snow most nearly approaches an ideal black body for longwave radiation, efficiently losing as well as gaining heat through this medium. When skies are clear, snow experiences a net heat loss to space by longwave radiation, the amount depending on the quantity of water vapor and carbon dioxide in the air, as well as the air temperature. Under overcast conditions, snow will lose heat by longwave radiation to clouds if the cloud temperature is lower than that of the snow surface. When clouds are warmer than the snow surface, the process is reversed and the snow gains heat by longwave radiation. This latter condition occurs most often in spring or summer, when the air and clouds are warm and the melting snow surface cannot rise above 0°C.

The effects of long- and shortwave radiation add algebraically to produce the net radiation balance of the snow surface. The net balance in winter is usually positive (snow gains heat) during the day and negative at night. Occasionally under clear skies at high altitudes in winter, when the sun angle is low, the outgoing longwave radiation may exceed the shortwave radiation absorbed by the snow even at midday, and the snow will actually be cooled while the sun is shining. Maximum positive radiation balance is achieved not on clear days, but under conditions of thin fog or low broken clouds in spring and summer, when both long- and shortwave radiation contribute heat strongly to the snow surface.

The exchange of heat in the snow cover by the medium of liquid water or water vapor has its greatest manifestation in the downward percolation of rainwater. This circumvents snow's normally low conductivity and can warm the entire snow cover, from ground to surface, to a uniform 0°C in a matter of hours.

AVALANCHE CHARACTERISTICS

LOOSE-SNOW AVALANCHES

Loose-snow avalanches arise when snow accumulates on slopes of steeper angle than its natural angle of repose. The snow on a given slope is made unstable by: (1) deposition of light, fluffy snow under conditions of little wind, (2) reduction of internal cohesion among the snow crystals by metamorphic changes, or (3) lubrication from percolating meltwater. When these conditions exist, loose-snow avalanches may release independently due to natural disturbances or due to small, artificial disturbances by skiers and mountaineers. Any small disturbance is propagated downward from crystal to crystal, causing the snow to slump downhill toward its natural angle of repose or, if momentum is attained, to slide onto slopes of lesser angle. The disturbance produces a chain reaction as more and more snow is collected in the sliding mass until sufficiently gentle slopes are reached for the moving snow to lose its momentum and come to rest.

The most dangerous loose-snow avalanches are those involving wet snow in the spring or summer. Often originating high on the mountains as true loose-snow avalanches, these may gather large quantities of snow by the time they reach the valley floor. The weight of wet snow gives them great destructive power even though their velocity may be low. Also, whether wet or dry, loose-snow avalanches can sweep skiers and mountaineers over cliffs, especially if the snow is underlain by ice, and are known to trigger larger, more dangerous slab avalanches as they descend.

SLAB AVALANCHES

The slab avalanche is of major concern because it forms the most important source of winter hazard in the mountains. Slab avalanches, in most cases triggered by the victims themselves, are responsible for the great majority of accidents. A snow slab is not exclusively associated with any particular type of snow crystal, and especially cannot be correlated with any visible snow characteristic. Wind is an important natural factor in slab formation, as wind-drifted snow commonly develops unstable slabs. But wind alone is not necessary to cause these dangerous slides—unstable slabs may develop through internal change in the absence of wind.

The tendency of a snow layer to slide depends not only on the character of that layer itself but also on its relation to adjacent layers and on the size and shape of the slope. Assuming that a given snow layer has sufficient internal cohesion to behave as a slab, whether or not it will slide depends on the mechanical character of its attachment to the mountainside. The primary anchorage of a snow layer is to its bed surface. The strength of the bond depends on the properties of the two layers, the nature of the bed surface, the temperature at the interface, the age of the bond, and whether a weak layer is sandwiched between the slab and bed surface. Gravity tends to pull the snow layer down the mountain. The primary condition of instability is reached when the stress exerted by gravity exceeds the strength of the bed surface anchorage. This may be achieved either by an increase in the stress (increased snow load or external load from mountain travelers) or a decrease in the strength of the bond (kinetic-growth metamorphism, crust disintegration, or meltwater lubrication as examples).

Weakness of the bed surface anchorage, however, is not a sufficient condition for a slide to occur, for a slab is also anchored at the sides, top, and toe. The strength of these anchorages must also be less than the stresses applied to them. The most important peripheral anchor is at the top, where the snow is subjected to tensile (stretching) stress; this is where rupture is most likely to occur following bed surface failure.

If all the forces acting to release a slab exceed the strength of all the anchorages, it will slide. In practice, only certain anchorages may be dangerously stressed, or some or all of them may be stressed close to but not exceeding the breaking point. Any outside trigger, which cuts or breaks part of the slab and then initiates a sudden redistribution of stresses, may break the anchorages and release an avalanche. The same thing can happen when a gradual increase in load or decrease in strength causes one of the anchorages to rupture; suddenly increased stresses are thrown onto the other supports and they too break. Failure propagation in the weak layer is thought to be the commonest initiator of slab release. If some of the anchorages are strong enough, they may sustain the slab, as in the common case of a snow slope that cracks but does not slide.

Under the force of gravity, snow on a slope is continually trying to move toward the valley, both by sliding on the ground and by internal deformation (glide and creep). It is the additional combination of stresses created by this glide and creep motion that gives to the slab avalanche its dangerously unpredictable and unstable character. When some triggering agent breaks a slab and relieves creep tension, the reaction of the snow may be very rapid. A whole slope may suddenly shatter into blocks before the slab has a chance to be set in motion. If the snow is very dense and cold, such as in hard slab, the release of tension may be signaled by a sharp cracking sound like a rifle shot. The propagation of a fracture line in snow that is subject to tension from heavy creep is extremely rapid. Such fractures may run faster than the eye can follow for many hundreds of yards across a slope.

If enough time is available and no triggers are present, the snow will eventually relieve or redistribute these stresses by internal deformation. The amount of time required depends on the viscosity of the snow. Snow near the freezing point can flow quite readily, and dangerous conditions do not persist for long periods. Thus, danger from warm snowstorms is usually of short duration and the snow quickly stabilizes. As temperature falls, the snow becomes stiffer and creep tension becomes more persistent. As noted above under "Formation of the Snow Cover," the progression of kinetic-growth metamorphism has a similar effect in stiffening the snow. This is the basis for the general rule that the lower the temperature, the longer the avalanche danger may persist.

Layering

The formation of unstable slab layers depends on discontinuities in the snow cover. A completely homogeneous snow cover—with an even gradation of density, crystal types, and other characteristics from surface to ground—would not likely form a slab avalanche. But each interruption of snowfall causes a change in snow characteristics from one layer to the next. The interface between two layers will usually have less strength than the layers themselves. Therefore, a snow cover with sharp discontinuities is a more likely source of slab danger than one that is homogeneous. Hard layers, such as rain crusts, are excellent sliding surfaces and are often the sources of repeated avalanche formation.

Moreover, between the bed surface and the slab layer, there often exists a weak layer deposited by light snowfall, graupel, or surface hoar sublimation. This provides lubrication for the slab through a weak shear bond at the bed surface. As a general rule, snow surfaces exposed to prolonged periods of weathering, no matter what the weather patterns may be, offer a poor bonding surface for a subsequent snowfall and hence often serve as bed surfaces for slab avalanches.

The variable distribution of snowfall and heterogeneous metamorphic conditions across a mountain slope create patterns of instability that influence triggering. Windblown snow can create an even blanket of stiff slab over a slope or accumulate in thick piles, commonly called *pillows*. Because the pillows add more stress to the underlying snow than thinner accumulations, triggering is common over the pillow. The transitions from sun to shade can also alter the viscosity of a slab, changing it from stiff and brittle in the shade to soft and malleable in the sun.

Although graupel can be evenly deposited as a layer, if it is cold and round it can roll off a slope to collect on benches. Once buried these collections of ball bearing–like crystals create an uneven pattern of weakness that may be difficult to detect. Surface hoar forms most readily where calm, cool air at night can pool and condense onto the snow surface, causing it to be most fully developed in the lower sections of a slope and in gullies and near streams. Also, surface hoar can be fragmented by wind and melted by sun. Like graupel, once surface hoar is buried the pattern of weakness and instability across a slope can be complex.

Small bushes accentuate temperature gradients and buried rocks create voids, both of which enhance kinetic-growth metamorphism. This creates patchy patterns of exceptional weakness that can underlie potential slab avalanches.

External Triggers

Many avalanche slopes reach a state of instability but never fall for lack of a trigger to effect final release. Common natural triggers exterior to the slab or loose-snow layer include falling cornices, rolling snowballs, lumps of snow falling from trees, icicles, rockfalls, or small slides. Sluffs that might otherwise be harmless frequently apply enough dynamic stress on the layers over which they run to dislodge larger avalanches. Large avalanches and cornice falls are especially effective triggering agents because they frequently carry enough force to bring down any layers that are not absolutely stable. Explosives are a form of artificial trigger frequently used to effect controlled release of avalanches.

Most avalanche accidents involve the unexpected release of snow slabs triggered by the victims themselves. No doubt many such avalanches never would have fallen had they not been artificially triggered.

How a snow cover responds to external forces depends on the visco-elastic properties of its layering. For example, wet-snow avalanches (both loose and slab) commonly are triggered from above their starting zones by sliding motions, such as glissading, snowplowing with skis or machines, or side-slipping down-slope with skis or snowboards. On the other hand, dry-slab avalanches can be triggered in a variety of ways. Soft slabs often are initiated by small disturbances near the top of a slope, such as a traversing skier or snowboarder. A stiff slab, however, may bear the weight of a person or sequence of persons for quite some time before its elastic strain energy builds to a point of failure and claims a victim. Fracturing can be at some distance from the triggering force. Also, slabs underlain by layers of kinetic-growth crystals can be triggered from many different places in or around the eventual fracture zone. This is because faceted crystals and depth hoar can propagate an initial disturbance over great distances, whereas other types of weak layers or weak interfaces under dry slabs typically fail within a small region around the point of disturbance.

The spatial variability of snow layering can cause delayed-action avalanches, ones that do not respond to an initial disturbance. Several snow travelers can be on and off a slope before the final trigger occurs. Two scenarios appear possible. In one, each traveler creates some disturbance in an underlying weak layer. This disturbance may add stress to the overlying slab. By themselves, however, the areas of added stress are not large enough to initiate tensile failure in the overlying slab. A final disturbance may link preexisting areas of weakened anchoring to cause slab failure. A second scenario suggests that the final traveler simply locates an area of increased stress, such as a wind pillow or convex

Figure 10. Typical avalanche terrain. Routes A and B are the safest. Routes C and D may be safe if snow conditions are stable. ▶

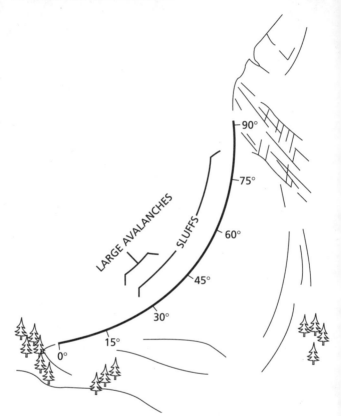

Figure 11. Although avalanches may start on slopes ranging from about 20° to 55°, most large avalanches originate in release zones between 30° and 45°. There is a strong concentration of avalanche frequency between 35° and 40°.

slope, or an area of enhanced weakness, such as a pocket of graupel or hoar crystals that previous travelers missed.

Internal Triggers

Internal triggers can include temperature changes, overloading by snowfall, and kinetic-growth metamorphism, any or all of which can alter the stress-strength relationships of a slab beyond its breaking point and so effect release. The operation of these agents is less obvious than the external triggers, but they nevertheless are responsible for the natural release of many slides. The most common internal trigger is fresh snow accumulation, which simultaneously builds a slab and stresses its anchors. The rate of overloading or deposition of a slab layer also is known to play an important part in avalanche formation.

TERRAIN

Steep gullies and open slopes are natural avalanche paths. Ridges, outcrops, and terraces are natural avalanche barriers. Ridges parallel to the fall line set definite boundaries to an avalanche path, while those running across the fall line halt, slow down, or divert the snow. Ridges also modify the flow of wind so that one side may be stabilized while the other is an accumulation zone for slab. As a practical matter, the windward edges of ridge crests provide the safest routes of travel through avalanche terrain, while rock outcrops may make effective islands of safety.

The most dangerous avalanche path is one with a broad release zone that funnels into a gully. This produces by

convergence a deep layer of flowing snow and high velocities. Open slopes produce lower velocities, but large, open
slopes permit fractures to run for long distances and very
large volumes of snow can be released as falling slabs. The
most dangerous avalanche paths in which to be caught are
those that run over cliffs or into timber, or that fall into
narrow gullies or catchment areas, where burial beneath
deep snow accumulations is likely.

Avalanche *accidents* occur on all kinds of terrain. Convex slopes, where creep increases tensile stresses, tend
to be active release zones, but many avalanches also release
on concave or plane slopes. The presence in a release
zone of a triggering agent (often the victim) is probably a
more important factor than slope profile. The slope *angle*
at the point of release is also important. Figure 11 sum-
marizes the typical range of angles at which avalanches
release. Although avalanches have been observed to start
on slopes as shallow as 15°, this is a rare circumstance
involving very wet snow (slush flows). Occasionally, dry-
snow avalanches will release on slopes between 25° and
30° but this is not at all common. Most large avalanches
start on slopes between 30° and 45° with a very pronounced
occurrence peak between 35° and 40°. People experienced
in avalanche control develop a keen sense for slope angle
and are able to discriminate high-risk angles from low-
risk ones. Less-experienced mountain travelers would do
well to check slope angles with an inclinometer until they
have learned to recognize the most dangerous angles.
Skiers often tend to overestimate slope angles by as much
as 10° or 15°.

Rough, irregular ground surface tends to retard slides until all the irregularities have been filled in by snowfall or wind drift. Smooth surfaces, such as grass, rock slabs, or ice, may permit avalanche formation with only a few inches of snow.

Knowledge of terrain is the key to avalanche safety. Accurate appraisal of snow conditions takes training, experience, and a good source of observational data, but the recognition of avalanche terrain can be easily learned. Safe winter travel in the mountains means, above all, safe routefinding. The avoidance of dangerous slopes, and especially the avalanche release zones, should become a matter of habit for ski tourers, snowboarders, snowmobilers, and winter mountaineers. The best way to learn safe routefinding is to travel in the company of an experienced avalanche worker. Illustrated slide lectures are also a good introduction. Learning by trial and error is the hard, possibly fatal way.

The subtle nuances of terrain recognition can only be learned in the field, but the basic principle is easy to summarize: stay off steep, open slopes. All too often, beginning students of snow and avalanches concentrate their attention on the details of snow metamorphism and internal snow-cover structure, hoping to be able to outguess snow conditions, when the first order of business is to master thoroughly the skills of safe routefinding in avalanche terrain. Again and again, avalanche accident reports are filled with such comments as "The victim took an unsafe line," "The accident party cut right across the release zone," "Mr. X entered the slope at the worst possible point," or, bluntly, "Only an idiot would have chosen such a route." Choose safe routes; it's the best way to stay out of trouble in avalanche terrain.

CHAPTER 2
Practical Guidelines for Stability Evaluation

THE EVIDENCE ABOUT SNOW STABILITY

The winter environment is full of evidence about snow stability, ranging from weather conditions to the actual fall of an avalanche. Not every kind of evidence has equal merit when it comes to judging snow conditions. Some kinds are easy to interpret, others much more difficult. There are three important classes of evidence:

Class I: Direct evidence about the mechanical state of the snow cover. This includes the fall of avalanches through natural or artificial release, propagation of fracturing in snow, snow cover collapse, and failure planes between snow layers initiated by test procedures.

Class II: Indirect evidence about the mechanical state of the snow cover. Most of this evidence is gathered by digging pits in the snow and investigating snow structure. Data include details like layering, slab structure patterns, crystal types, water content, and mechanical strengths.

Class III: Information about meteorological conditions that build the snow cover. These include the commonly observed weather factors like wind, temperature, precipitation, humidity, and cloudiness. Features like new-snow density and crystal type, snowfall intensity, and metamorphic changes also fall into this category.

CLASS I: DIRECT EVIDENCE ABOUT THE MECHANICAL STATE OF THE SNOW COVER

1. **Avalanching.** The most reliable evidence about unstable snow is the fall of an avalanche, either witnessed or deduced from observing debris or a fracture line. This may seem obvious, but it needs stating. It is surprising how many beginners are found in an ostrich-like position scrutinizing snow crystals with a hand lens while concrete evidence of snow behavior goes ignored.

   An avalanche seen falling says there is danger *right now*. Fresh debris tells of recent instability that may still persist. Older evidence needs more thought. Has the danger period passed, leaving the snow now stable? Or has the older danger been followed by new instability? Crown faces still visible at fracture lines suggest that paths may not yet have been reloaded by new snowfalls. No avalanches at all, especially after a big snowstorm, raises a warning. Has the snow stabilized, or are the avalanche slopes lying in wait for a trigger?

2. **Cracks or fracture formation.** When unstable snow, especially a soft slab, is disturbed, cracks will often

propagate for some distance, even on level ground. This is a key indicator of slab avalanche conditions. When such cracks cross the release zone of an avalanche path, a slab may fall. Snow cracks limited to the immediate vicinity of a ski track may not be a sign of danger, but when such cracks shoot out ahead of the skis for 5, 10, or even 15 meters, it's time to stay on safe ground.

The experienced winter traveler constantly checks for this condition by taking every opportunity to disturb the snow. Kicking a miniature cornice on a gully, the casual flick of a ski pole against a snow cushion, or an extra stamp of the foot on a slope only a meter or so long are all ways to see if the snow is under tension and will propagate cracks. Absence of cracking is not a guarantee of no avalanching, but its presence is a serious warning sign.

3. **Sounds of rapid settlement.** A weak layer in the snow cover, often depth hoar, can offer poor support to the layers above. When such snow is disturbed, it sometimes collapses with an audible "whumpf." This kind of snow settlement, even on level ground, warns of danger. Similar settling on or in the vicinity of a steep, open slope can easily trigger an avalanche. *Beware of snow that "talks" to you!*

4. **Mechanical tests.** Among the simple mechanical tests used to locate failure planes (shear surfaces) in an unstable slab, the simplest is the "shovel test" (Figure 12A). To conduct the test, excavate a pit on a slope of at least 30° to the desired test depth, then

Figure 12. Testing an isolated column of snow approximately the width of a shovel blade (about 30 cm on a side): A) shovel test—place a shovel behind the column and gently pull the handle forward; B) stuff-block test—load the column with a stuff sack full of snow or blocks of stiff snow; and C) compression test—load the column by gently pressing down with the shovel blade.

excavate in the wall of the pit a column of snow on three sides, each about the width of the shovel blade (30 cm or so). Cut the back of the column with a snow knife or string to obtain consistent results. Working down from the top, insert the shovel at the back of the column and gently pry outward. Watch for the formation of failure planes. Small shovels are fine, larger ones with a flat blade are better, and a snow knife makes cutting out the snow column faster and easier. An "easy" failure versus a "medium" or "hard" one is a matter of subjective judgment. Often the effort to cause shear failure is less significant than the quality of the failure. There is a greater likelihood of widespread instability if failure occurs rapidly, causing a block to slip off the test surface, leaving a smooth plane or gouging into a deep layer of depth hoar. Instability typically is more localized if the failure plane is uneven. If the shear plane fails under its own weight without shovel help when the column is exposed, the snow is definitely unstable. Be careful.

To estimate how much weight is required to cause failure, pile an isolated column of snow with blocks or bags of snow (stuff-block or *collapse test*) or apply pressure to the top of the column with a shovel blade *(compression test)* until failure occurs (Figures 12B and C). While quantitative values may be helpful in determining the degree of instability, they are imprecise measures that vary widely across a slope. Finding stable conditions in tests of an isolated column does not mean that the entire slope is stable.

Figure 13. The Rutschblock test—isolate a large block of snow approximately the width of skis (about 2 meters on a side). From the top of the block, slowly add the weight of a skier, who jumps until release.

The Swiss introduced a way of enlarging the test column to more closely approximate slope conditions with the Rutschblock test (Figure 13). In this test, a column that is the approximate width of skis (about 2 meters) is excavated on three sides from a slope of at least 30°. Many avalanche professionals recommend cutting the back of the column, before adding a load, by sawing with a string or cutting with a detached, upturned ski. However, snow commonly contains wind-hardened layers or thin crusts, making it difficult for strings to slice through and for skis to cut through smoothly. Therefore, it is useful to learn how to perform the test with a three-sided column. That way, the tensile strength of the potential slab and the shear strength of the underlying weakness are tested simultaneously, as occurs in an actual avalanche, and they are reasonably replicated because of the large size of the Rutschblock column.

If failure does not occur under the weight of the block alone, a skier moves onto it, parallel to the back end. If failure still does not occur, the skier jumps once, then twice. Finally, a person jumps onto the block without skis. Stability is considered poor if failure occurs before the skier jumps once and is considered fair if failure occurs after that. Variations of the test may be accomplished with a snowboard or by diving onto the slab with limbs extended. Like column tests, however, the quality of shear plays an important role in determining instability from a Rutschblock test. Fast, clean failures are more indicative of instability than partial or uneven failures. Also, although the sample size is much larger than an isolated column, snow layering remains highly variable and a stable result from a Rutschblock test is no guarantee that an entire slope is stable.

None of the above tests reasonably locate very fragile weaknesses that can occur in the upper layers of soft snow. These types of weakness commonly trap mountain travelers shortly after storms in seemingly

Figure 14. Modified tilt test to locate very weak shear planes in new snow: A) lift a pie-shaped wedge out of the snow that is thick enough to include the most recent snowfall layer(s), then B) tilt the shovel slightly and gently rap the bottom until failure occurs.

small avalanches that can become deadly. For this reason, it is useful to adapt the tilt *board test* (Figure 14), which is commonly applied in study plots by Canadian avalanche forecasters. To perform this test in the backcountry, slice a large pie shape out of the face of a snow pit with a shovel or snow saw, roughly the dimensions of a shovel blade. Remove the pie piece with your shovel a few centimeters past the thickness of the most recent snowfall, then tilt the shovel slightly and gently rap the bottom. If failure occurs as you tilt the sample or after one or two gentle raps, expect unstable conditions.

For the novice observer and for observers new to a region, it is important to build test columns that reach to the ground (old firn snow on a glacier surface or a thick rain crust may act as a ground interface). While this is relatively easy to accomplish in shallow snow covers, it is no less important in deep snow covers. The crown faces of deadly, skier-triggered avalanches have been as small as a few centimeters to well over 3 meters.

Absence of failure planes does not guarantee stable conditions nor does their presence assure that an avalanche will fall. But an easily dislodged layer bond in the snow cover is a serious warning sign.

Caution! Although mechanical tests are most informative when done in locations near actual release zones, do not conduct them in dangerous terrain; work on a safe slope. The tests examine snow structure by creating a miniature slab failure; take care not to create a full-scale specimen.

CLASS II: INDIRECT EVIDENCE ABOUT THE MECHANICAL STATE OF THE SNOW COVER

Most of this evidence is gathered by digging pits in the snow; it includes the following:

1. **Thickness of snow cover.** Thickness, the simplest characteristic of the snow cover, tells a lot about stability. A shallow snow cover, usually less than 1 meter, can experience strong kinetic-growth metamorphism and set the stage for later avalanching by losing mechanical strength. Deep snow, on the other hand,

favors equilibrium metamorphism and increasing stability with time, but it fills or covers terrain irregularities, which inhibit avalanche formation, and hence favors surface slab formation.

2. **Slab configuration.** The slab structure is a combination of layering that puts at least moderately cohesive snow on top of a favorable sliding surface, a weak layer, or a combination of both. The slab layer can range from soft, new snow to old, settled wind slab with the consistency of concrete. The avalanche-forming slab configuration does not depend on any specific *kind* of snow in the slab layer. It depends on the proper *combination* of slab, weak layer (failure plane), and sliding surface. A snow pit's key function for checking stability is to locate slab structure patterns.

The weak layer may be low-density new snow, surface hoar (very common), some graupel to serve as ball bearings, or a water-saturated layer in wet snow. Sometimes no distinct weak layer can be seen in the pit wall, but a poor bond between one snow layer and another may still exist. Mechanical tests can help locate weak layers and bonds.

The sliding surface is often a buried crust or ice layer. It may be an old, smooth, windblown surface or simply a snow layer with a higher density and strength than the slab above. The sliding surface of a previous avalanche is also a good candidate. Sometimes, especially with wet-snow avalanches, the sliding surface is the ground and the slab is the whole snow cover. Many cold-snow avalanches *start* by sliding *on* weak depth hoar but end up sliding on the ground, when their motion causes the depth hoar to collapse.

3. **Snow crystal types.** The different types of snow crystals are also useful indicators of snow stability. Fine-grained, settled old snow (equilibrium metamorphism) tends to be stable if it extends throughout the snow cover, though it can still build slabs if a sufficiently weak layer lies underneath. *Kinetic-growth crystals in any state of development are universal warning signs.* Such snow means loss of strength and gain in viscosity (stiffness), both of which contribute strongly to slab avalanche formation. Depth hoar, the end product of this metamorphism, is always a danger sign, and at the very least it makes snow behavior difficult to predict. Fresh loading on depth hoar by snowfall or wind drifting generates dangerous instability whose exact character is very difficult to evaluate. When depth hoar is around, be careful!

4. **Mechanical strength.** The mechanical strength of snow, such as its hardness, gives useful information about snow cover behavior. A surprising amount of information can be obtained just by digging a snow pit. One's kinesthetic sense, or "feel," of how snow reacts to a shovel is a rich source of knowledge about snow strength and texture. In many cases, all the rest of the observation routine to log layer characteristics may just be window dressing; the key information may be obtained by the time the digging is finished.

   Snow produced by equilibrium metamorphism has a solid, cohesive feel. Snow with kinetic-growth crystals, on the other hand, has a more friable texture that disintegrates more easily and tends to be brittle even when soft. Poorly consolidated, often unstable snow shovels easily and can be scooped up or broken with little effort. Snow settled enough to gain strength and stability is more difficult to shovel. Each shovelful has to be spaded or pried loose.

The fine points of the kinesthetic sense are difficult to convey in print, but experience quickly makes the differences clear. The habit of digging frequent, shallow, quick snow pits to check surface conditions, coupled with close observation of stability (Class I data), is one of the best ways to gain a confident understanding of avalanche formation.

5. **Temperature.** Temperature affects snow behavior in many ways. Some are subtle, requiring careful measurement and interpretation. Others are obvious and provide much of the important temperature information about stability.

The biggest temperature distinction is whether the snow is cold (subfreezing) or at the melting point with some liquid water present. Cold snow does not change very fast; at low temperatures avalanche danger may persist for a long time. Close to the melting point, but still subfreezing, the snow changes rapidly, and high avalanche danger does not last long. With meltwater or rain present, many snow characteristics change so quickly that metamorphic processes are short-circuited. In wet snow, extreme avalanche danger may develop quickly but usually does not last more than a few hours.

Strong temperature gradients within the snow cover warn of declining snow strength. Their effects may not become evident immediately, but they show a *trend* toward instability. The effects of temperature gradients are most pronounced in early winter; they diminish toward spring, as the snow cover warms.

CLASS III: INFORMATION ABOUT METEORO-LOGICAL CONDITIONS THAT BUILD THE SNOW COVER

1. **Snowfall.** Snowfalls are the key meteorological evidence for avalanche formation. The bigger the snowstorm, the bigger and more likely the avalanches. Twenty centimeters or more of new snow is always a warning sign. One meter in a single storm is getting down to serious avalanche business, and really big blizzards that dump 2 meters or more in a very few days can generate large avalanches everywhere. Even more important than the quantity is the rate of fall, or *snowfall intensity (S.I.)*. When slopes are loaded quickly, whether by precipitation or wind drifting, the snow cover cannot adjust fast enough to the new burden. As a result, instability rapidly increases. Even a substantial amount of snow, up to a meter or more, may not cause much danger if it falls over a long time. The critical loading rate for the common soft slab formation seems to be around 2.5 centimeters of snow per hour.

2. **Precipitation intensity.** An even better measure of loading is *precipitation intensity (P.I.)*, the rate of snow

accumulation measured in its water equivalent (the amount of water that would result from melting the snow). The critical P.I. is about 2.5 millimeters of water equivalent per hour. Any sustained snowfall above this rate accompanied by high winds practically guarantees some sort of avalanching.

3. **Precipitation type.** The kind of crystals that make up a snowfall also can affect avalanche formation (see Figure 6 in Chapter One). Ordinary stellar or dendritic crystals do not particularly favor large avalanches unless they are broken and packed by the wind. When coated with rime, they are much more likely to build soft slabs; fully developed graupel (pellet snow) can build dangerous slabs in thick layers or lubricating layers in thin ones. Crystal types like needles or plates, which pack to higher densities, favor slab formation. In fact, any kind of snow crystals that create atypical new snow densities can favor avalanching. Typical densities run around 10% water equivalent. Below about 5%, the very light snow tends to slide off as loose sluffs, whereas densities above 12% to 15% contribute strongly to building dangerous slabs.

4. **Wind.** Wind controls the distribution of snow on the mountainside. Wind loading on lee slopes is a prime cause of high snowfall intensity and snow depths, hence of avalanche formation. The critical velocity for dangerous wind transport is around 5 to 10 meters per second (m/s), varying a bit with snow type. Winds of 10 to 20 m/s are avalanche builders. Above 25 m/s in

colder climates avalanches are much less likely to form; most slopes become either scoured or heavily wind packed. In coastal areas with warmer climates and wet, heavy snow, major storms with hurricane-force winds can lead to serious avalanching. Wind direction is very important because it determines *which slopes* will be loaded and where cornices will form.

5. **Trends and change.** Air temperature and humidity affect the kind of snow crystals formed during storms. Air temperature and radiation conditions (see "Thermal Properties of the Snow Cover" in Chapter One) also control the heat balance of the snow surface. Many temperature effects on snow are complex and difficult to interpret. A few, however, are simple. A rapid change in air temperature, either up or down, affects stability. A sudden, sharp cooling can put thermal stresses on hard slabs. Such a temperature drop from above to below freezing can trigger wet-snow releases as it first occurs, followed by stability as the snow freezes solid. A sudden rise from subfreezing to melting frequently provokes avalanches if the initially cold snow was weak and unstable to begin with. The temperature trend during a snowstorm is important. A falling temperature brings with it decreasing new snow density and a more stable snow deposit. A rising temperature, on the other hand (the so-called "inverted storm"), brings initial low snow densities to form a good failure surface for the subsequent higher-density accumulation, the ideal soft slab configuration. The air temperature at or just

before the onset of snowfall is also important. New snow bonds poorly to a previously cold surface, but sticks much better to relatively warm though still subfreezing snow.

An important general weather factor in avalanche formation is *rapid change* of any kind. A sudden onset of a snowstorm, changes in temperature as noted above, a shift from snowfall to rain, or high winds springing up to cause rapid loading of lee slopes are all warnings of avalanche development. A quick change in wind direction or velocity during a storm, an abrupt change in snow crystal types, a shift in radiation conditions as clouds move in or out, all can cause or set the stage for avalanches. Always be alert to sudden weather changes in the winter, consider what the effects will be on the snow cover, and proceed with extra caution when a stable weather period of any sort comes to an end. Pay special attention to the onset of rain or rapid thaw conditions, for these produce the most profound changes in previously cold snow. Rain in midwinter can change safe slopes to deadly ones in a matter of minutes.

THE CHAIN OF CAUSE AND EFFECT IN AVALANCHE FORMATION

In any given area the terrain is fixed and determines *where* avalanches can fall. *Whether* and *when* they will fall is determined by a chain of cause and effect that runs from the weather systems that generate snowfalls through the complex evolution of snow cover structure to the final mechanical state of loads and weakness, stresses and strains, that determine the degree of instability at a given time and place. The observer follows this chain by observing nature from Class III through Class II to Class I evidence about snow stability. The farther one gets down this chain, the more direct and unambiguous is the evidence: Class I data come closest to answering the question "will it avalanche" with a simple YES or NO. The warning signs are clear and easy to interpret. Moving back up the chain to Class II data, the answer is more often a "maybe," and the questions begin to multiply. A wider range of factors, such as slab structure, failure planes, and relative layer strengths have to be weighed against one another. Backing up even farther, to Class III data, the many nuances of wind, snowfall, temperature, crystal types, radiation effects, and their interactions together form a complex network of cause and effect. The same question has to be answered, "well, perhaps if . . . ," or "not unless X is followed by Y," or "probably, if A, B, and C occur, but not D."

The lesson is clear. The difficult decisions about snow stability are best made when based on Class I data. (This is why ski patrols in developed ski areas spend so much time using bombs and artillery; the answers thereby obtained about snow stability are 98% unambiguous.) Increase the data uncertainty (Class II, or even more so, Class III), and the answers start getting fuzzy. Evaluations become more general and less specific: "A rising hazard may occur in the Southern Rockies by tomorrow night." The fuzzier the answers, the wider the safety margin that must be allowed in practical decisions.

Ideally, stability evaluation should focus on the least uncertain class of evidence. In the real world, some data from all classes are usually considered, with the balance of emphasis shifting according to locale, season, and snow patterns. Sometimes the evidence from one class is overwhelming. A meter of new snow overnight, no matter what else happens, practically screams "avalanche." Depth hoar so fragile it flows out of a pit wall like dry sand tells of a snow cover on the point of collapse. The really big hazard situations are often obvious. It is the condition of marginal stability that so often traps the unwary skier and that requires careful analysis. Recognizing avalanche danger is always a synthesis of many kinds of evidence, some of it not always consciously perceived. The principles of this synthesis, along with some practical rules, are outlined in the next section of this chapter.

ANALYZING THE EVIDENCE
THE NATURE OF AVALANCHE FORECASTING

A stability evaluation deals with the *current* state of the snow cover but coupled with weather forecasts, it attempts to foresee *future* avalanche conditions. In either case, the act of evaluating, or forecasting, snow stability should be *an ongoing process,* not a last-minute or one-time event. The skier who is about to cross an avalanche path and suddenly decides to investigate snow conditions with a pit, think about weather effects, or scan the horizon for recent avalanches has started the process too late . . . much too late. At the very minimum, conditions should have been considered before the tour started that morning. Better would have been two or three days, or even a season, of paying attention to weather developments.

Accurate knowledge about snow conditions is built up bit by bit, adding a little meteorology here, some snow stratigraphy there, salting the mixture with a few shovel tests, and stirring it to form tentative conclusions that can be checked against actual avalanche occurrence. The experienced forecaster is always thinking about snow conditions and considering how today's weather may change them tomorrow. The experienced forecaster *always has an opinion about snow stability,* no matter how uncertain or tenuous, which can be checked against actual snow behavior and modified by further observations. As emphasized earlier, this modification proceeds most accurately when based on Class I evidence, but where this is not available, Class II or Class III evidence is sought. The farther back up the chain of cause and effect one must go, the more diverse and numerous must be the data to improve the stability opinion. The evaluator is always looking for extra information, one more bit of evidence to reinforce or disprove the snow stability estimate. In Chapter Four, examples of actual stability analyses by experienced hands make this process clear.

THE TWO PROBLEMS IN AVALANCHE FORECASTING

There is a useful distinction between absolute and conditional instability of the snow cover. *Absolute instability* means the snow has reached a point where widespread natural avalanche releases *will* occur. The conditions producing this state are usually obvious, such as a big storm with a lot of new snow, a sudden onset of rain in midwinter, or a severe episode of depth hoar formation followed by strong wind drifting. Even beginners have little trouble predicting what is going to happen in such circumstances. Much more difficult to deal with is *conditional instability.* This means that a slab avalanche structure has formed in the snow cover but will actually generate avalanches *only when an adequate triggering force is supplied.* Evaluating stability then becomes much tougher, for the key question then becomes: "How big a triggering force is needed?" If only an earthquake or large explosion will dislodge the snow, it is stable for practical purposes. But if the weight of a skier can start a slab moving, the danger is obviously high. Yet the external appearance of the snow cover may be the same for both cases. This is the heart of the matter: *A really reliable decision about the actual danger during conditional instability can only be made on the basis of Class I information.* Anything else is a probability estimate, guesswork of varying reliability. For absolute instability, Class II and Class III data will do the job because the probabilities are overwhelming. But if the situation is conditional and you don't know the trigger size required, allow a wide safety margin and get more information from observed avalanche falls, test skiing, or evidence of fracture propagation. In the case of key decisions (e.g., to cross an avalanche slope or not), even mechanical tests begin to assume Class II uncertainty.

When approaching the challenge of a stability evaluation, the first question to ask is which of the two problems are you facing: absolute or conditional instability?

SOME BASIC RULES ABOUT SNOW

1. Any snow or weather condition that departs from normal may decrease snow stability. An important corollary is that any departure from the normal course of equilibrium metamorphism in the snow cover can set the stage for slab avalanches.

2. Absolute instability occurs only a very small percentage of the time, typically for a total of a few hours each winter. Conditional instability can persist much longer, as long as several weeks in cold climates when depth hoar is in the snow cover.

3. The exposed snow surface breeds instability. Weathering of the snow surface adversely affects the bonding of the next snowfall. The longer the period of weathering, the worse the bond.

4. Formation of wet-snow avalanches in the spring usually is governed by the *net* heat balance at the snow surface. This balance is determined by several factors, not just by sunlight (see Chapter One).

5. *Most avalanches are caused by a rapid change in the thermal or mechanical energy state of the snow cover.*

SOME BASIC RULES ABOUT EVALUATING STABILITY

1. Avalanche forecasting is an evolutionary process. Each forecast, each stability evaluation, ideally begins with the first snowfall of winter.

2. It is not difficult to recognize a general pattern of unstable snow in a given mountain area. Doing so rapidly becomes more difficult, however, as the area of

concern narrows down to a specific avalanche path at a specific time.

3. Class I data are the easiest to interpret. Class II data are more complicated. Class III data are often open to many alternative interpretations. The best way to beat confusing data is by building redundancy, i.e., by gathering more than one line of evidence about snow stability.

4. There is a fundamental asymmetry to understanding avalanches. It is much easier to recognize conditions leading to 100% certainty of avalanches than it is to recognize that the snow is 100% stable.

SPECIFIC SITUATIONS
SOFT SLAB AVALANCHES

Soft slabs involve low-density, and hence mostly new, snow. They form as a direct result of snowfalls and can quickly reach dangerous instability, which, however, normally does not last long. Soft slab avalanches usually involve surface layers of new snow and are directly associated with fresh snowfalls. They are probably the commonest source of danger in the mountains. *Beware of soft slab avalanche danger during and after big winter storms.* If temperatures remain only a few degrees below freezing, the snow stabilizes rapidly, often accompanied by visible signs of settling. At lower temperatures the danger can persist longer, even for days.

Many snowstorms do not produce soft slab danger in the absence of certain other key weather factors. The most important of these is high precipitation intensity. More than

25 millimeters of water equivalent (around 25 cm of snow) falling at rates of 2.5 millimeters per hour or more, accompanied by strong winds, reliably produces avalanche danger. Heavy (high-density) new snow is especially avalanche prone. If the storm deposit falls on a deep snow cover with a smooth surface, soft slab formation can be widespread, sometimes with little regard to wind direction below timberline. Heavily rimed snow crystals strongly favor dangerous soft slabs. Unrimed crystals tend to build very shallow layers and can act as weak layers below soft slabs.

Extensive sluffing during a storm stabilizes avalanche slopes and inhibits slab formation. Midstorm sluffing may not always be visible because it is obscured by later snowfall. Soft slabs are especially amenable to ski testing because the ski tracks penetrate the slab layer and disrupt it. From this standpoint, soft slabs can be recognized from Class I evidence without much difficulty. Experienced observers can often recognize soft slab snow conditions just on the basis of the "feel" while skiing, even without actual fracturing or avalanche release on test slopes. The Class III evidence, such as the precipitation and snow type effects outlined above, also are reasonably easy to interpret. It is the Class II evidence that gives little help in recognizing soft slab conditions. The slab structure patterns in new snow can be so subtle that they go unrecognized in a pit wall or lie outside the measuring range of typical test instruments.

HARD SLAB AVALANCHES

Of all avalanche types, hard slabs are the most dangerous and unpredictable in behavior. Such snow is strong enough to support appreciable load or withstand weak triggering forces without release. Dislodgement may occur unexpectedly on slopes on which previous skiing or other disturbance has failed to have any effect. This contrasts with the more "touchy" behavior of soft slabs, which usually are stabilized or released by skiing. Hard slabs are particularly sensitive to temperature changes, and a sudden fall in temperature may greatly increase their instability.

The primary agent in developing hard slabs is snow transport by high winds. Average wind velocities of 10 to 20 m/s are commonly associated with this form of hazard. Strong wind transport can create very heavy lee deposition zones during light snowfalls, or even during fair weather. It is not uncommon to find slabs 2 meters thick forming in a few hours. This same heavy wind transport of snow tends to localize the hard slab danger on favorable lee slopes, in contrast with the more ubiquitous soft slab danger.

The weak layers underneath hard slabs that form the failure planes frequently consist of depth hoar or old, buried surface hoar. These make hard slab conditions especially difficult to analyze, for failure can occur unpredictably. The high mechanical strength of thick, dense snow layers that make up a hard slab favors strong anchorage to the terrain. Even with a very weak layer underneath, such snow may support a heavy accumulation built up over an extended time before failure actually occurs and an avalanche falls. This is a very difficult situation to recognize, because no class of evidence about snow stability tells very much. Class III data may be stretched out over time and therefore difficult to interpret unless an overwhelming event like major wind drifting occurs. Class II data may give useful information such as an obvious depth hoar layer, but deep, hard snow offers practical obstacles to an easy pit excavation, and when a pit is dug, the failure plane can be overlooked if it is thin and indistinct. Even Class I data is not of much help in evaluating hard slab danger. Actual hard slab releases tend to be erratic indicators; ski testing is ineffective; slab cracking is difficult to initiate; and shovel tests are impractical. *Do not expect ordinary ski testing routines to reveal hard slab danger.* Some serious avalanche accidents have happened through misunderstanding this principle. The most reliable way to check hard slab danger is to blast the slope in question with a heavy charge of explosives, though even this is not 100% certain.

A hard slab with an unstable failure plane located deep within the snow cover is the most difficult avalanche situation to deal with. Careful attention to all the evidence can point to instability, but reliable conclusions are difficult to reach. When a hard slab is suspected, the best policy is to play safe and practice conservative routefinding to stay away from release zones.

WET-SNOW AVALANCHES

Wet-snow avalanches typically fall when free water lubricates or weakens snow layers with some latent instability. Meltwater or rain is a very efficient transporter of heat through the snow and deep snow layers may be quickly warmed up when sufficient water is available. Wet-snow avalanches also can occur when the air temperature warms rapidly from below freezing to above freezing with the onset of heavy rain. This loads an already weak snow cover, causing avalanches at the beginning of the rainstorm, well before rainwater penetrates to deeper layers.

Wet-snow avalanches may fall either as slabs or as loose snow, depending on snow conditions, but the primary cause is the sudden intrusion of a large amount of water on top of or into the snow. Winter rainstorms are one source of wet avalanche danger, and are common in the maritime climate of the Pacific Coast ranges. Melting by solar radiation, warm winds, or both, is another cause. Melting due to radiation depends on the net radiation balance. During clear, dry weather, longwave radiation cooling of the snow surface tends to counteract the heat from the sun, and late winter or spring snow may remain stable during clear days, only to develop a wet avalanche cycle on a warm, hazy or cloudy day, when the net radiation heating of the snow is higher and may persist all night as well as during daylight hours.

Wet-snow avalanche danger is most acute when heavy melting or rain introduces free water into a cold, dry, and poorly consolidated snow layer. Hence late-season snowstorms are apt to be followed by a wet slide cycle, especially on south-facing slopes, if the next day is sunny. Deep falls of new snow in midwinter that turn to rain at the end of the storm are a similar source of danger.

A layer of depth hoar at the bottom of a snow cover may cause large, wet ground avalanches in the spring, when percolating meltwater reaches this unstable layer and further weakens it, while at the same time reducing the strength properties of the overlying layers.

Sunballs rolling down a slope are indicators of rapid changes taking place in the snow. They may be forerunners of wet slide activity, though not always. The danger usually is not high if the sunballs are small and penetrate only a few inches into the surface layer. But if these balls grow in size during the day and eventually achieve the form of large snow "wheels" that penetrate deeply into the snow, then wet-snow avalanching may be imminent.

Impervious layers in the snow cover, such as an old rain crust, favor wet-slab formation by trapping meltwater where it can provide extra lubrication.

Old, settled snow, or summer firn snow, is much less likely to cause wet slides. Snow that has been warmed up to the freezing point for some time is usually well stabilized and able to resist the effect of percolating water.

AVALANCHE DANGERS IN SUMMER MOUNTAINEERING

At high altitudes, winter avalanche conditions persist into summer. In addition, summer mountaineering presents its own hazards.

1. Old summer snow, or firn, normally is highly stable. Snow avalanche danger (as contrasted with that from ice avalanches) usually results from summer snowstorms. Warmer air and intense solar radiation can cause much more rapid changes following a storm than occur in winter. Damp- or wet-snow avalanches—both loose-snow and slab—may follow a fresh snowfall. The danger from damp or wet slabs may in some circumstances persist for several days, even in warm weather.

2. Wet-snow avalanche activity will cease when the snow freezes on a clear night (even with air temperature above freezing). These avalanches may fall at any time on overcast nights, or in wet, rainy weather, for the snow then does not freeze.

3. The bergschrund at the head of a glacier sometimes serves to create a slab avalanche fracture line, presumably due to the additional stresses introduced by glacier motion.

4. Snow avalanches on a glacier offer a peculiar source of hazard, for even a small and otherwise harmless slide can carry a climber into a crevasse and bury its victim very deeply. Consider carefully the possible consequences before risking a crossing of an avalanche slope with crevasses below.

5. When climbing cliffs or steep gullies, beware of hidden snowfields above, which may discharge unexpected slides, especially on a sunny afternoon.

6. At higher elevations, prolonged snowstorms may create winter snow conditions and typical winter avalanching in midsummer. In such situations the previous general outline of winter avalanche formation applies. The principal modifying factor is the much greater heat available in summer from solar radiation.

7. In the high mountain ranges of Alaska or the Himalaya, winter is truly present year-round, and snow avalanches must be expected at any season. A peculiar hazard arises from the great size of the avalanches that may fall from these huge peaks. Such avalanches may fall many hundreds of meters from

entire mountain faces and run for kilometers across glaciers or valleys below. Such slides have been observed to ascend the opposite mountain walls for hundreds of meters. Selecting campsites safe from such avalanches is sometimes difficult.

8. Ice avalanches belong to a separate category. They occur on the steep ice cascades of glaciers or under hanging glaciers and ice cliffs. The location is usually restricted and usually obvious, except in poor visibility. Their fall, on the other hand, is often impossible to predict, for collapse of a tottering serac or the fracturing of an ice cliff depends as much on glacier motion as it does on such processes as internal melting. Zones of frequent avalanche activity are usually apparent from broken ice debris of previous falls. Unlike snow avalanche accidents, in which the slides are usually started by the victims, ice avalanche accidents generally result from a natural fall. The basic safety precaution, therefore, is to minimize exposure to the hazard. Climbing parties should traverse passages beneath ice avalanche zones as quickly as possible. Avoid bivouacs or rest stops in such exposed zones. There is sometimes a reduction of ice avalanche activity at night, when the ice freezes up, but this is often not the case when glacier motion is vigorous.

CHAPTER 3
Safety Rules and Rescue

MINIMIZING AVALANCHE RISKS

When traveling in avalanche terrain:

1. *Never travel alone.*
2. Always conduct the march in such a fashion that only *one person at a time* is exposed to avalanche danger. This is the *first cardinal rule* for ski touring, and one too often neglected. If one person is buried by an avalanche, chances of rescue may be good if companions are free to search for the victim or go for help. If an entire party is trapped by an avalanche, its chance of survival is greatly reduced.
3. Stay off avalanche paths and, especially, out of release zones. This is the *second cardinal rule* for ski touring. Accident records show that *most avalanche victims start the avalanches themselves.* Cases where unsuspecting victims have been overwhelmed by a slide falling naturally from above are very much in the minority. *The safest route* around an avalanche path is over the

Figure 15. Basic equipment for traveling in avalanche terrain (transceiver, shovel, collapsible probe).

top, along ridges. The next safest route is along the valley floor, at the foot of the avalanche path. The *most dangerous route* is on the avalanche path, where the passage of a skier may trigger the release of an avalanche that otherwise would not have occurred.

4. Do not camp, bivouac, or make rest stops at the foot of an avalanche path. The probability of getting caught by a natural fall rises rapidly when exposure is prolonged. The chances of getting caught while you are moving are very much smaller.

5. On winter tours in the backcountry, every member should carry an electronic transceiver (rescue beacon), a shovel, and a collapsible probe (Figure 15).

6. The greatest danger exists during or immediately after a heavy snowfall or prolonged periods of high wind. Stay out of hazardous areas at these times. (Danger may persist for many days if temperatures are low.)

7. Do not assume a slope is safe just because it did not slide when the first person crossed it. Especially in the case of hard slabs and low temperatures, avalanche release may be triggered unexpectedly at some later time, even after considerable traffic on the slope. There is one case on record where an avalanche trapped the thirty-third man of a military patrol crossing a dangerous slope. In another case, a fatality occurred when the late-afternoon release of a hard slab trapped a victim on a slope that several skiers had used as a ski run all day.

8. Beware of lee areas, the slopes beneath cornices, and deep drifts, especially those with a convex profile. These are all prime locations for avalanche fracture zones.

9. Do not assume that avalanches are confined to open slopes. Dense timber is usually good protection, but open or scattered timber stands may not necessarily hold the snow. This is particularly true in the Rocky Mountain region, where depth hoar formation is common in early winter. Several avalanche fatalities in Colorado have resulted from release of slab avalanches on timbered slopes.

10. Most dangerous avalanches originate on slopes between 30° and 45°. Be careful on slopes within this range.

11. When you set forth on a tour, take advantage of local knowledge of snow and avalanche indications. Call

the nearest avalanche center for the latest information based on the most complete snow and weather records available. Professional ski patrol members or forest and park rangers often can give you locally specific information.

12. Test skiing is an attempt to artificially release avalanches on selected small slopes by skiing. It serves as a field test of snow stability to check the conclusions of hazard forecasting. The reaction of snow under skis constantly provide information on the physical processes taking place in the snow cover. Test skiing can detect snow that is tending to form slabs and create an impending hazard, particularly during storms. A key to successful test skiing is the selection of test slopes which accurately represent the snow conditions found on the larger and more dangerous avalanche paths. Cracks that form in the snow with the passage of skis are the best indicators of developing slab avalanche danger. Breaks in the snow immediately adjacent to the skis are not necessarily a danger sign; the weight of the skier may simply be cracking the snow locally. Breaks or cracks that run ahead of the skis are more clearly a warning of slab avalanche formation. *Warning!* Test skiing is one of the most useful tools for detecting avalanche danger, but it can be hazardous if done carelessly. The following precautions are mandatory:

- Work only on small, short slopes with a safe outrun.
- *Never* test ski alone.
- Only *one* person on the test slope at a time.

- Always cut slopes at the top.
- Do not attempt test skiing unless you are a competent skier.
- Adopt the safety precautions outlined on the following pages.
- Remember that test skiing is most effective in soft, surface slabs—it may not work in hard slabs. Deep, unstable layers in the snow, like depth hoar at the bottom of a hard slab, may remain undisturbed by passage of a skier on the surface, but still cause a major slab release later on.

13. Crossing an avalanche slope in the backcountry involves a certain calculated risk. You may be unable even to guess whether or not the slope will slide, but you usually can estimate *what will happen to you if it does slide* while you are on it. Taking a calculated risk may be justified if the slope is short and not likely to bury you deeply at the bottom. But if the slope is long, funnels into a gully instead of fanning out, falls over cliffs, or would carry you into rocks or trees at the bottom, the risk may be more foolhardy than calculated. Ask not only "will it slide?" but also "what will happen if it does slide?"

14. Any travel in avalanche terrain involves some risk. Keep this risk to a minimum and always play the odds in your favor. If there is a choice of two different routes, take the least dangerous one, even if both seem to offer low hazard. A lot of seemingly small risks, if repeated, can add up in the avalanche's favor. One chance in a hundred of getting caught may seem a small risk. But if you

repeat this one hundred times, the odds become
something like 6 to 4 in favor of the avalanche; repeat
a risk of two chances in one hundred a hundred times,
and the odds in favor of the avalanche increase to about
7 to 1. Old hands at snow-safety work learn this principle
so well that they take the safest line in avalanche terrain
even when they know the snow is stable. This is a good
rule for all winter travelers in the mountains.

If you must cross an avalanche slope:

1. Remove the wrist loops of your ski poles.
2. Unhitch the safety straps from your skis so they won't
   be tied to you if you are carried down in a slide. If
   your bindings are of the nonrelease type, loosen them
   so you can get out of your skis easily.
3. Close up your clothing, don hat and mittens, and raise
   your parka hood. If buried in the snow, your chances
   of survival will be much better if snow doesn't get
   inside your clothes to cause chill.
4. Loosen the straps of your rucksack so it can be
   dumped quickly if necessary.
5. Make sure by audible check that all transceivers are
   working in the transmit mode. Also make sure that
   they are securely attached inside your clothing,
   where forces generated by the avalanche will not tear
   them away. Wear an avalanche cord if one is available.
   Tie one end to your belt and let it trail out behind you.
   If you bring down a slide, the cord has a good, though
   not guaranteed, chance of floating on the surface even
   though you are buried.

6. Gain some measure of security by climbing or descending the fall line on foot instead of traversing the questionable slope on skis. A fall line track is less likely to cut a slab anchor than is a diagonal or horizontal ski track. In highly unstable situations, there may be little to gain by going on foot, and the mobility offered by skis in deep snow may recommend them in spite of the risk of cutting the slope. Wallowing through chest-deep snow in the middle of an avalanche path is not an experience to be relished.

7. Take advantage of natural protection offered by the terrain. Rock outcrops, clumps of trees, or ridges may offer islands of safety in the avalanche path. Lay your route between these and, if on skis or snowboard, try to make rapid downhill traverses that will carry you to the next safe spot even if the snow does start to slide.

8. Cross a suspected slope so that *only one party member at a time* is exposed to avalanche danger. The other members should watch the person crossing so they can plot his probable course in case a slide is started and he is swept down and buried.

If you are caught in an avalanche:

1. Call out so other members of your party can observe your course in case you are buried.

2. Discard poles, skis, and rucksack.

3. Try to swim in the snow in order to stay on the surface. Try also to work your way to one side of the moving snow. In a large or fast-moving avalanche such

efforts will probably be of little avail, but they may save your life in a smaller one.

4. If you find these efforts are not helping, cover your face with your hands. This will help keep snow out of your nose and mouth, and allow you to clear a breathing space if you are buried. As the avalanche slows down, try to maintain some space around your chest to allow respiration. Avalanche snow often becomes very hard as soon as it stops moving. Your chest may be constricted and your arms pinned wherever you find them when the snow comes to rest.

5. If you are buried, try to avoid panic. Frantic and fruitless efforts to free yourself will only consume valuable oxygen. Stern self-control is essential to survival. *Be confident that your transceiver is working and that your comrades know how to use theirs to find you.*

6. In soft snow you may be able to dig yourself out, or at least make room to breathe. If you try to dig out, make sure you dig up toward the surface. Persons buried in an avalanche have actually lost their sense of direction and tried to dig down. Also be aware that while you may hear sounds from the surface very clearly, rescuers can seldom hear you. Snow is an effective sound insulator. Although this insulating quality works in both directions, into and out of the snow, the *perception* of sounds by buried persons and by those on the surface is entirely different owing to the large difference in background noise.

7. Many avalanche survivors are rescued immediately by their companions because they have a hand, foot, or

piece of equipment protruding from the avalanche debris. If you think you are coming to rest near the surface, try to reach out a hand or thrust up a foot (but keep one hand free to clear space around your nose and mouth).

RESCUE BY SURVIVORS

In his book, *The Avalanche Enigma,* Colin Fraser remarks that "to be in an avalanche is to have at least one foot in the grave, and more usually both." Statistics fully bear him out. Worldwide, in a sixteen-year period ending in 2001, over 2,200 people have died in avalanches. While Switzerland, France, and Austria maintain the highest avalanche fatality rates, with annual deaths up to 50 at times, the United States is catching up. Between 1995 and 2000 an average of 26 people died each year by avalanche in this country. In that period, 31% of the fatalities were snowmobilers, 21% were skiers, 16% climbers, 14% snowboarders, and the rest were workers, homeowners, motorists, and other recreationists.

Even more instructive are the survival statistics. In Switzerland, where the records are most complete, 1,347 people survived partial or complete avalanche burial over a recent thirty-year period, an average of 45 per year. Of these, 39% dug themselves out, 34% were extricated by survivors on the scene, and only 27% were recovered by organized rescue actions. The central fact is that people die very quickly when buried under snow (Figure 16). The successful rescue is the speedy one, and time lost means lives lost no matter how well organized or equipped the survivors or rescue parties are.

Figure 16. Percent of survivors as a function of burial time for completely buried avalanche victims. From the Colorado Avalanche Information Center.

If someone is buried in an avalanche, prompt rescue operations are the only hope of getting the victim out alive. There are records of persons living several days while buried, but such instances are exceptional. Ordinarily the victim either is killed by mechanical injury, or dies within a short time from shock and suffocation. Some victims die within a few minutes from no obvious cause.

Two-thirds of avalanche fatalities are due to suffocation. Most of the remaining third are due to mechanical injuries, mainly to the head or neck.

Earlier statistics suggested that about 50% of completely buried victims were still alive after the first hour. In recent years the rapidly expanding record of accidents exposes the mournful fact that the 50% survival time is actually closer to 30 minutes. The chance of survival drops to less than 20% after 2 hours. Less than a third of completely buried victims are recovered alive.

Depth of burial is also critical. For burial depths of less than half a meter, the survival rate is around 45%. Only 1% survive burial at depths of more than 2 meters; at more than 3 meters there are no survivors.

Rescue operations that seek at least a 50–50 chance of success must therefore locate *and uncover* the victim within a half hour. Once more the emphasis: *speed is crucial.*

But remember too, these figures are averages and exceptions can always occur. Special circumstances, like being trapped in an air pocket, can prolong a buried victim's life far beyond the averages, so rescue operations ought not to be abandoned until all reasonable hope of success is past.

Because time is such a critical factor in surviving an avalanche, the best hope for any victim is to be recovered quickly by members of their own traveling party. For this reason, while electronic transceivers (rescue beacons) used to be considered a luxury required only by extreme skiers, they now are a necessity for anyone willfully entering avalanche terrain, including ski tourers, snowshoers, climbers, snowboarders, and snowmobilers. Other basic equipment to be carried by each person includes a shovel and collapsible probe.

The time required for a searcher to cover an area of 10,000 square meters (about 2.5 football fields) with a transceiver is less than 15 minutes. An experienced transceiver searcher can succeed in about 5 minutes. By contrast it typically takes 20 people nearly 4 hours to cover the same size area with a coarse probing pattern.

RESCUE PROCEDURES

Memorize these ten steps. If you are a surviving member of a party caught in an avalanche, the lives of your buried comrades may depend on what you do in the next few minutes.

1. **Don't panic.** Check for further slide danger—pick a safe escape route in case of a repeat.
2. **Mark last-seen point.** Mark the point on the avalanche path where the victim was last seen carried down by the snow. This will narrow the area of your search and that of the rescue party. Use a firmly planted ski, pole, or large branch that will not be lost under a subsequent snowfall.
3. **Switch transceivers to receive.** Double-check that all survivors have turned their transceivers to receive. Only the victim(s) should be transmitting.
4. **Quick visual search.** Survivors must make a quick but careful search of the avalanche before beginning a thorough search.

- **Search surface below last-seen point.** Search the surface of the avalanche for evidence of the victim or clues to his or her location. Mark the location of any pieces of equipment you may find—these may provide additional indicators of the path taken by the flowing snow. Search carefully and kick up the snow to uncover anything that may lie just beneath the surface.

- **Search most likely burial areas.** Follow the general flow line of the avalanche; check above and below trees, rocks, or other obstacles in the path. Look near the toe of the debris pile, at the lateral edges of the avalanche, and in depressions where snow may collect.

5. **Quick transceiver search.** Spread the survivors out into a search sweep of parallel lines less than 20 meters apart and less than 10 meters from the edge of the avalanche debris. The fastest search occurs if terrain and party disposition after the accident permit a downhill search parallel to the fall line. Maintain a constant distance between searchers as you descend the avalanche path, never advancing more than 20 meters at a time. Use a zigzag pattern to maximize spacing.

6. **Sole survivor.** If you are the sole survivor, you must still make a thorough search of the avalanche before going for help. This may seem obvious, but it is a rule all too often neglected. Even the simplest search may enable you to find the victim and free him or her alive.

7. **Thorough search.** Survivors must concentrate on making as thorough a search as possible with their own resources. The chances of a buried victim being recovered alive diminish rapidly after the first half hour.
   - **Thorough transceiver search.** More than likely a transceiver signal will be detected during the quick search, at which time call out that you have received the signal and begin a bracket (grid) or tangent (induction or flux) method of search as described in the following section "Transceiver Search Procedures."
   - **Probing.** If the initial search fails and the victim or other party members do not carry transceivers, begin probing with the heel of your ski, inverted ski pole, or collapsible probe below the last-seen point. Trees, ledges, benches, or other terrain features that have caught the snow are most likely places to search. If there are several survivors, probing of likely spots can continue until a rescue party arrives. If you are alone, you will have to decide when to break off the search and seek help, depending on how far away it is.

8. **Send for help.** If there are several survivors, send only two. The remaining survivors must search for the victim in the meantime. If it will take a half hour or more for help to reach the site, and if the avalanche is not too large, the victim may have a better chance if everyone remains to search. This is a difficult decision that depends on individual circumstances.

9. **Going for help.** When going for help, travel carefully,

avoiding avalanche dangers and injuries from trying to go too fast. The victim's chance of survival may depend on your getting through. Mark your route, especially if fresh snow is falling, so you can find your way back. Try to avoid complete exhaustion. The rescue party normally will expect you to guide them back to the accident site unless its location is absolutely clear.

10. **Care of the victim.** When the victim is found, immediately give first aid for suffocation and hypothermia. Free the nose and mouth of snow, clear the chest, and administer mouth-to-mouth resuscitation unless the victim is able to breathe freely without assistance. Cardiopulmonary resuscitation should be applied in the absence of breathing and pulse, only by those trained in its use. It should not be interrupted once begun. Clean out snow from inside the clothing and place the victim in a sleeping bag with external sources of heat. Persons buried for any length of time in snow are apt to suffer severely from hypothermia and will need effective rewarming. Other injuries should be treated according to standard first-aid practices.

TRANSCEIVER SEARCH PROCEDURES

The *bracket method* of transceiver search employs a grid pattern to locate the maximum transceiver signal. The *tangent method* follows an electromagnetic flux pattern that the transceiver emits. Both methods require only a few minutes to locate a victim's signal. A *pinpoint search* pattern is required

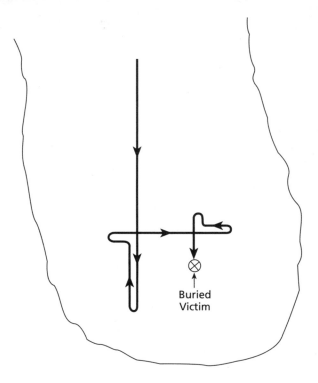

Figure 17. Bracket method of transceiver search.

before digging. All methods of transceiver search require practice at least every winter, but preferably before each trip.

Bracket search method. This method can be conducted with any type of electronic transceiver.

1. Orient the transceiver in your hand by turning or twisting for the best signal (loudest tone, maximum number of lights, and/or minimum distance reading).
2. If your transceiver has volume or light control, reduce the signal to the lowest detectible level.
3. While holding the transceiver in the best orientation, continue forward until the maximum signal is reached. It usually will be necessary to go past this maximum point until the signal falls off, then return to it by retracing steps along the search line.
4. Determine by excursions in both directions at right angles to the initial search line which way the signal strength continues to increase, and move along a straight line in that direction until the signal maximum is again located.
5. Repeat the procedures again, moving at right angles to the second search line. This will usually bring the search very close to the victim.
6. Continue until the signal decreases toward all directions, then begin a pinpoint search pattern (described below).

Tangent search method. This method requires more practice but commonly is faster than the bracket method. It is easiest with digital transceivers that have dual antennae but can be performed with any single-frequency 457 kHz transceiver (see "Technical Aids to Locating a Victim" later in this chapter for a discussion of equipment).

1. With the transceiver pointing forward, turn your body to obtain the best signal (loudest tone, maximum

Figure 18. Tangent method of transceiver search.

number of lights, and/or minimum distance reading).
2. If your transceiver has volume or light control, reduce the signal to the lowest detectible level.
3. Walk in the direction that the transceiver is pointing about five steps or 5 meters.

If the signal becomes weaker, go about 5 meters in the opposite direction.

4. Reorient your body for best signal and follow the transceiver direction another 5 meters.

5. Repeat steps 3 and 4 in 5-meter increments until the signal decreases in both forward or backward directions, then begin a pinpoint search pattern (described below).

Pinpoint search method. Avalanche debris can be extremely compact and difficult to shovel. Being off by even a few centimeters can delay a successful rescue. Also, the transceiver on a deeply buried victim can cause a large area of maximum signal at the snow surface. Therefore, it is important to pinpoint the victim before digging. First, mark the area of maximum signal, then begin a pinpoint search with a fine probe or bracket or tangent transceiver search.

1. **Pinpoint probe.** This offers a fast, effective way of pinpointing victims. It is preferred by many experts and is the best pinpoint method for novices. From the middle of the area of maximum signal begin probing in an expanding spiral pattern.

2. **Pinpoint bracket.** Remove the transceiver straps to hold it close to the snow and orient for the best signal. Maintain the orientation while conducting a small grid pattern until the signal decreases toward any direction.

3. **Pinpoint tangent.** This method requires a great deal of practice and experience and is most successful with a single-frequency, digital, 457 kHz transceiver with dual antennae. Remove the transceiver straps to hold

it close to the snow. Refine the directional aim of the transceiver by tilting it into the snow. It may help to twist the transceiver 90° to see the flux alignment from the side.

Multiple burials. If more than one victim is buried with transceivers, searchers may hear two or more competing signals. Try to concentrate on one signal at a time, locate it, and then work toward the next one. Whenever possible, turn off the transmitting signal once it has been located. Pulse rates of different brands may be distinguishable. If the victims are buried far apart, different searchers may pick up the signals at different strengths and the problem will be quickly resolved. If the victims are buried close together, sorting the signals may require a slower scan of the snow surface to pinpoint individual locations. Backup work with avalanche probes may be necessary for closely adjacent victims.

1. Follow the strongest signal (lowest distance reading) with a bracket or tangent method, as described above, until the closest transceiver has been isolated and pinpointed.
2. Uncover the first victim and turn off their transceiver if possible.
3. If you are alone, quickly clear the first victim's airways, check for vital signs, then resume searching for the next victim.
4. If there are multiple survivors, assign one or two to administer first aid to the first victim while all others resume searching for the next victim.

ORGANIZED RESCUE ACTIONS

If the victim cannot be found by comrades, then an organized rescue team must be called. While backcountry travelers are not likely to organize a formal rescue themselves, it is not uncommon to be involved as an accident survivor or simply as a bystander in the area. Therefore, it is helpful to understand the line of command and standard procedures.

Successful avalanche rescue operations depend on trained leadership, staffing, special equipment, and, above all, organization. Successful (and by definition, speedy) rescues can seldom be improvised on the spot. Proper equipment must be provided and organization established beforehand. Although volunteer staffing can often be recruited in an emergency, rescue teams must be led by persons who are trained in rescue techniques. Leaders must know how to sound an accident alarm, and where to locate volunteers and equipment. They must know the designated rally points where volunteers can be assembled and equipped. They should know details of the local terrain and the normal areas of avalanche hazard.

The rescue leader often is the most experienced person in an area. He or she does not necessarily lead by marching at the head of a rescue party, but by providing the organizational nucleus that holds a rescue operation together. The leader cannot function adequately without lines of communication—telephones, radios, megaphones, runners. He or she appoints column leaders for rescue columns moving into the field, and ordinarily also designates one of the column leaders to be accident site commander. The latter directs the rescue measures at the accident site, unless for some reason the rescue leader decides to assume this function him or herself.

Organized avalanche rescue proceeds in three distinct stages.

STAGE ONE—LOCATION AND RECOVERY OF THE VICTIM

Speed is the essential factor during this stage. Competent rescue personnel should reach the accident site with all possible haste. Subsequent organization of medical and logistical support is begun only after the first rescue parties have been dispatched.

1. On receipt of an accident alarm, the rescue leader calls for first-stage volunteers and appoints leaders for these groups. If the accident site is known accurately, the first groups leave immediately with all possible speed, equipped with probes, shovels, headlamps, and, whenever possible, rescue transceivers for their own protection as well as for victim search.

2. If witnesses remain at the accident site to guide the search groups, additional staffing is dispatched there as fast as it becomes available. If the person bringing word of the accident is the only witness, he or she should be returned to the site as fast as his or her physical condition permits in order to point out the victim's approach to the slide and the last-seen point.

Figure 19. Fine and coarse probing techniques to search for a buried victim. ▶

EXECUTION OF THE FINE PROBE

EXECUTION OF THE COARSE PROBE

3. At the avalanche the accident-site commander assumes charge of the search operations. He or she directs a search of the debris surface for clues and to mark key locations, such as the last-seen point. If the victim is known to be carrying a transceiver, the accident-site commander also directs an electronic search. He or she also initiates probing operations, when appropriate. The exact manner in which these will be done depends on the peculiarities of the avalanche, the number of buried victims, and the number of searchers at the site commander's disposal.

4. Once a quick visual check for clues has been completed, the rescue party begins coarse probing in the most likely locations. The coarse probe (Figure 19) moves rapidly. It is intended to locate the victim quickly at those depths of burial where he or she has the most chance of survival. If staffing permits, more than one coarse probe line may be in operation. These lines move fast enough to uncover clues to the debris surface as well as to probe for the buried victim.

5. Initial probing activities usually will concentrate on the most probable areas of burial, such as around trees, boulders, or other obstructions; where changes in slope occur; and at the tip and edges of the debris. If the last-seen point has been clearly marked, the search will further concentrate in the natural flow line downhill from this point.

6. The coarse probe does not guarantee locating the victim alive at a given spot, but statistical analysis shows that the increase of speed over the fine probe

improves the victim's chance of survival. The fine probe virtually guarantees the victim will be found if not buried below the probe depth, but there is a much greater chance that the victim will be found dead. Analysis further shows that the victim's chance of survival is also better if the coarse probe is repeated when it fails on the first sweep. The statistical advantage of the coarse probe over the fine probe increases as the size of the search area goes up.

7. Because the fine probe is so much slower than the coarse one, it will normally be introduced only after the chances of live rescue have become small. Fine probing may take several hours to cover the likely burial spots in a large avalanche. It is usually intended to recover a body rather than to rescue a living victim.

8. With either type of probing, a separate shovel crew normally follows the probe line. If a strike is made, the probe pole is left in contact with the buried object, while the rest of the probe line moves on. The shovel crew then digs out the strike without interrupting the continued search, thus wasting no time if the strike does not turn out to be the victim.

9. Normal precautions during the rescue include posting an avalanche guard if danger from other slopes still exists, dispatching or radioing reports to the rescue leader on search progress and needs, and maintaining a close control over search parties to ensure that searchers do not fall exhausted, become lost, or wander into an avalanche danger zone. This last precaution is especially important at night.

10. The preceding steps assume the rescue team will travel on the ground to the accident scene. In many areas helicopters are available, which greatly improve the speed of rescue. They also improve safety by transporting the rescuers without exposing them to avalanche danger en route, although care must be taken when approaching the accident site because it is possible for the downdraft from the helicopter rotor to start other avalanches in unstable snow. Trained rescue groups can benefit from practice with helicopter transport to ensure maximum safety and minimum lost time during an actual rescue. Helicopter evacuation of recovered victims is especially valuable because they can often be taken directly to a hospital. As demonstrated by current experience, the combination of radio communication, electronic rescue transceivers, and helicopters can lead to very rapid recovery of buried avalanche victims. In some cases, though, the record of live recovery has improved little owing to the time required to dig out deeply buried victims. The victim's best chances still lie with immediate recovery by the survivors on site as soon as the avalanche comes to rest.

STAGE TWO—FIRST AID AND TRANSPORT OF THE VICTIM

1. As soon as the Stage One columns have been dispatched, the rescue leader organizes a first-aid column, which should include a medical doctor whenever possible. This column carries first-aid and

resuscitation supplies, shelter, sources of heat, and facilities such as a toboggan to transport the victim. Allowing for extra time to open central caches, procure equipment, and collect personnel, the first-aid column must also move with speed. Prompt, effective first aid is almost as essential to the victim's survival as his or her disinterment from the snow.

2. Because suffocation is a major medical factor for avalanche victims, the provision of resuscitation equipment is necessary. Mouth-to-mouth resuscitation is the first step to revival and should be applied as soon as the victim's head and chest are uncovered. Be careful at this point; mechanical injury of the head and neck may be present and could be worsened by rough handling. Prolonged artificial respiration is exhausting to the operator, especially at high altitudes. Modern, hand-operated resuscitators provide more reliable and controlled ventilation of the victim's lungs with intubation, but do have limitations. At low temperatures common to avalanche rescues, icing may give trouble with the valves. Much more important, the resuscitator pumps cold external air into the lungs and causes further chilling of an often hypothermic victim. Equipment to deliver warmed, humidified air for field treatment of hypothermia is a very useful adjunct to avalanche rescues. Oxygen may also be supplied (the resuscitators usually have a fitting for this), but is not essential except at very high altitudes. Prompt and steady artificial respiration is the essential provision.

3. Current medical opinion in the United States and Europe recommends cardiopulmonary resuscitation (CPR) for avalanche victims who exhibit absence of both breath and pulse. In this situation, prompt, steady application of CPR without interruption is important. CPR should be done only by persons trained in the technique, and training in CPR should be undertaken by as many prospective members of a rescue party as possible.

4. All victims recovered from avalanches should be assumed to suffer from hypothermia and handled accordingly. Once a victim is recovered with breathing and pulse restored, the danger is not over. Hypothermia poses a threat that persists after excavation from the snow. Body temperature may continue to fall during transport, possibly cooling the heart to a point where fatal fibrillation may occur, as cold blood from the extremities mixes with warmer blood in the body core. Allowing a victim to walk speeds this process and may result in collapse. Beware of this "rescue death."

In profound hypothermia the victim's heart is very sensitive. Rough handling may cause it to function improperly or stop beating completely. Gentle treatment is essential. Remove wet clothing carefully (cut it off if necessary) and if possible, place the victim in a prewarmed sleeping bag or otherwise insulate from the cold. Insulated external heat sources may be placed near the neck, armpits, groin, or kidneys; hot sources must never be in direct contact with the skin.

If breathing and pulse are lost during transport, continue resuscitation efforts until the victim has reached a hospital. Many victims who appear pulseless while cold have been successfully resuscitated once warm.

All winter travelers in the mountains should learn the hazards of hypothermia and the correct ways of dealing with them. Any avalanche rescue is likely to involve hypothermic persons, quite possibly among the rescuers as well as the victims!

5. Once the victim has been revived, or breathing restored, he or she must be watched carefully for subsequent cessation of breathing or pulse. Resuscitation in this case must be initiated immediately. Mechanical injuries are handled according to standard first-aid techniques. Transport follows normal procedure for winter accident victims.

6. Provision of adequate first-aid and resuscitation supplies in rescue caches builds the foundation for successful rescue work. (See Appendix A: Avalanche Rescue Caches.) The care and handling of the victim after recovery cannot be too strongly emphasized. The rescuer's job is only half done when the victim is found.

STAGE THREE—LOGISTICAL SUPPORT FOR PROLONGED RESCUES

1. In the event of a deeply buried victim, several victims, or a large avalanche, the search may become prolonged. Additional support for the rescue workers will be needed. Once the rescue leader has dispatched the search and first-aid columns, attention can turn to

organizing relief staffing, supplies of food and clothing, transport (e.g., helicopters or oversnow vehicles), better lighting for night work, and reliable communications with the accident site. Such work normally brings the rescue action under the cognizance of civil authorities.

2. Systematic fine probing is arduous work, especially in hard snow, and is destructive to all but the stoutest probe rods. Provision of relief for the probing parties is necessary if the search is prolonged. Adequate supplies need to be delivered to the site. There normally is some leeway in organizing such support, but even so, the first relief groups should be arriving at the accident site within 2 or 3 hours after the first rescue columns.

3. If systematic fine probing fails to locate the victim, then trenching of the snow is usually necessary. This is a major shoveling operation, which can go on for many hours, or even days. It obviously is aimed at recovering a body rather than effecting a live rescue. Trenches are dug parallel to the slope contours down to ground level or to undisturbed snow. The walls between the trenches are probed laterally. Normal trench spacing is 2 meters, but this can be increased to 3 if sectional probes are available. Digging can also begin at the tip of debris cones and proceed uphill. It is best to space the shovel crews along one trench, with frequent reliefs. In this way snow from one trench can be thrown into the one just completed.

TECHNICAL AIDS TO LOCATING A VICTIM

The time-honored methods of mechanical detection—the probe and avalanche cord—remain useful because of their simplicity. The avalanche dog is a superb search "device," but requires a complex organization for training, maintenance, and delivery to be effective. Electronic rescue transceivers have dominated search technology in the last two decades for practical and technical reasons, but above all because they enable an *immediate search by survivors for a buried victim.*

Portable search radars that detect reflections from a buried body have been built, but they are difficult to use because they also detect many spurious reflections. If the victim carries a radar transponder (frequency-doubling diode), search radars are much more effective. A radar system based on transponders has recently been introduced in some locations. A strong permanent magnet can readily be detected by a portable magnetometer, but the method has not gained wide favor owing to the high cost of this instrument and its limited search range.

The need for speed presents a basic, practical limitation for any complex device that must be transported from a central rescue station to an accident site. Any such device, no matter how effective, is more valuable in saving a rescue team's time in locating a body than it is in saving a life.

AVALANCHE DOGS

A well-trained avalanche dog, usually a German shepherd, is often a very effective means of locating a buried victim in many cases and is the only fast method for a victim who carries no signaling device. In Switzerland, more than 27% of live victims in recent years have been located by dogs, more than by any other single method. But an extensive network of trained dogs, coupled with efficient transportation, is necessary for such success. In North America, the record of dog rescues is limited. Many past efforts here to train good avalanche dogs have failed because of the extended time and systematic effort required. More recently, a nucleus of good avalanche dogs has been developed largely through the efforts of search and rescue dog associations. Nevertheless, the big North American problem with avalanche search dogs remains one of transporting them to often remote accident sites in time to effect live rescues. On this continent, most successful dog searches to date have recovered dead bodies.

Even untrained dogs sometimes will instinctively seek out buried victims, especially if the victim is the dog's master. Rescue groups are well advised whenever possible to take along any robust, winter-conditioned dog.

Avalanche survivors can contribute to rescue success by keeping a search dog's capacities and limitations in mind. A trained dog can do a coarse search at the rate of about 20,000 square meters (about five football fields) per hour. It will locate most live victims regardless of burial depth or snow conditions. It will locate dead victims in porous snow up to 2 meters deep and in compact snow up to 1 meter deep. A dog may have trouble immediately after an avalanche comes to rest because the victim's scent takes a few minutes to diffuse through the snow to the surface. Normal foot traffic by searchers on the avalanche debris does no harm, though it is helpful to clear the search area a few minutes before the dog arrives. Other odor sources in the snow, such as buried animals or household debris, may distract the dog. (Do not urinate on the avalanche!)

Consult local ski areas or rescue-dog associations for current information on available trained dogs. The location and telephone contacts for local avalanche dog handlers can be prominently posted in avalanche caches to help speed rescue.

THE AVALANCHE CORD

Following an avalanche cord is one means of locating an avalanche victim. The cord is commonly light in weight, made of red or orange nylon, and about 15 meters long. The traveler in avalanche terrain attaches one end around his or her waist and lets the full length of the cord trail behind. The theory is that at least some part of the cord will float to the surface of the avalanche as it comes to rest and thereby provide a visible sign of the buried victim's location. Some commercial cords have small metal arrows attached every meter or so to indicate which end of the cord to seek. A recent advance includes a ball that is formed by a series of hoops in nylon segments that fold against the back of the traveler's rucksack. The wearer deploys the avalanche cord and ball by means of a rip cord loop that is in front of a waist belt.

Avalanche cords do work, but they are not infallible, as some tests using dummies in real avalanches have proven. The cords have the advantages of simplicity, low cost, and reliability. Their disadvantages are inconvenience in use and a tendency to get tangled up with other party members, other avalanche cords, or trees and bushes. The latter problem is severe for a fast-moving skier below timberline. Part of the tangling problem can be minimized if the cord is carried rolled up like a ball of yarn and deployed when approaching avalanche terrain. This is done by tossing the ball to unroll it after the free end is attached to the bearer. In recent years the avalanche cord has been widely supplanted by electronic rescue transceivers, but for safe winter travel it remains a useful alternative whose "batteries" never run down. A long piece of stout nylon cord also has many uses for the winter traveler.

AVALANCHE PROBES

The avalanche probe is a long, slender rod which enables a searcher to kinesthetically feel differences in resistance (mechanical permeability) between snow and buried victim. (For information on executing search procedures with probes, see "Organized Rescue Actions" earlier in this chapter.) Also, probes are needed to pinpoint the location of victims found by transceiver or dog.

Collapsible probes are a valuable adjunct for any backcountry winter traveler. A sturdy probe for occassional backcountry use consists of aluminum alloy or carbon fiber tube sections strung on a coated stainless steel cable with a tensioning device at one end. The outer tube diameter should be 10 millimeters or less and the extended length should be 3 meters. Most probes of this type collapse to less than 40 centimeters for easy packing. Beware of very thin, lightweight probes because they may break easily in avalanche debris. Ski poles that convert into probes by removing baskets and screwing together are handy but their thickness and tapered shell make them difficult to push and pull in and out of avalanche debris.

Full-length probes, usually 3 to 4 meters long, are the standard equipment of rescue caches. They are usually brought into play when prolonged searches must be made, often in dense, hard avalanche debris. They must be stiff and strong, but not so large in diameter that pushing them into hard snow exhausts the rescuers. *Avoid aluminum probes* for this purpose. While aluminum alloy is adequate for occasional backcountry use, repeated experience has shown that the material will not stand up to prolonged work in hard snow. Especially avoid aluminum electrical conduit. Any serious probing in the debris of a real avalanche will quickly turn conduit into a pile of pretzels. The best probes are steel, preferably tempered thin-wall steel tubing, or carbon fiber, with an outer tube diameter of about 10 millimeters or less.

Probes can be hazardous to the buried victim. In soft snow the resistance of a human body can be readily felt by the prober. In very hard snow the "difference in mechanical permeability" of a body and the surrounding snow is slight. Cases exist where probing failed to find a victim who later was recovered by trenching and found perforated. Chances of serious injury to the victim can be reduced, though not eliminated, by providing blunt tips on the probes.

ELECTRONIC TRANSCEIVERS

Electronic transceivers (rescue beacons) carried by persons exposed to avalanche danger transmit an electromagnetic signal that can be picked up by another transceiver that is switched to the receive mode. The transmitting unit is located by tracking increases in the received signal strength. These devices afford a fast, effective means of locating someone buried in avalanche debris, Today they are universally used by snow safety professionals and backcountry travelers including skiers, winter mountaineers, snowmobilers, snowshoers, and snowboarders.

As of 1995, the frequency of 457 kHz has been adopted as the international standard for rescue transceivers. Some older models transmit and receive on a frequency of 2275 Hz, and some models transmit both frequencies. While the problem of incompatible frequencies has diminished in recent years, especially in North America and western Europe, some countries and private clubs continue to use surplus transceivers at the old frequency. Therefore, it is imperative that traveling parties ensure that all members are transmitting and receiving on the same frequency and that rescue caches include dual frequency transceivers.

All transceivers transmit and receive pulsed radio signals. The less expensive analog transceivers simply convert the inaudible transmission into an audible tone that echoes the strength of the original pulsed signal. Transceivers that digitally receive the signal transform it into visual and audio output. The visual output helps when wind or other noise is a problem and the digital values can show directions and approximate distances to the transmitting signal. The downside of digital beacons is that their shorter range may outweigh their ease of use and increased accuracy. Each product has a unique pulse rate, which is useful when locating signals in multiple burials. Generally, a faster pulse rate is easier to locate than a slower pulse rate. Newer digital transceivers include dual antennae, which facilitate tangent-method searches.

Rescue transceivers have already saved the lives of several avalanche victims, but they do not guarantee survival. The mountain traveler should have a clear understanding of what they can and cannot do. Rescue transceivers are a simple, effective, and reliable means of *locating another unit operating in the transmit mode.* They offer no guarantee that such a unit will be recovered attached to a live body. Accident records include several cases where the buried victim's position was determined within a few minutes by a rescue transceiver, but the dead body was only recovered after hours of shoveling. Some common-sense precautions when using rescue transceivers can greatly enhance safety in avalanche terrain:

1. Make sure the units have fresh batteries properly installed or an internal battery fully charged.
2. Set the unit to "transmit" and turn it on. When a party sets out, check each unit by listening to it with another unit set to "receive." This check at the start of each tour is important!
3. Carry the transmitting unit inside a shirt, suspended around the neck or otherwise securely attached close to your chest, not in a pocket. A high-speed avalanche can remove a surprising amount of clothing; be sure

the transceiver is not apt to go with it. A unit carried in the rucksack is useless, for the rucksack is one of the first things you want to get rid of when caught in an avalanche.

4. Each person carrying a transceiver should also *carry an avalanche probe.* A survivor can switch his or her unit to "receive" and locate a buried victim's position within about 1–2 meters. The system will not tell how deep the burial is or give the exact place to start digging. Once electronic location of the victim is accomplished, probe for the precise location and then dig down along the implanted probe.

5. Each person carrying a transceiver should also *carry an adequate shovel* (see "A Special Note on Shovels," below). The importance of this rule cannot be overemphasized. You may locate a buried avalanche victim with great dispatch, but this affords little comfort if you have only your hands or the heel of a ski to dig with. The portable shovels commonly used for winter mountaineering and ski touring are much better than bare hands.

Practice the search procedure regularly. Don't wait until one of your party is buried to figure out how the rescue transceivers work. Follow the printed search technique furnished by the manufacturers of these units. Although these techniques differ in minor details, they all employ a systematic search pattern, which closes in on the buried transmission with minimum lost motions. Do not run around at random on the avalanche debris; this can waste valuable time. (See "Transceiver Search Procedures" earlier in this chapter.)

A SPECIAL NOTE ON SHOVELS

A variety of lightweight shovels are available for personal packing. Because the chance of successfully locating victims with transceivers is so great, carrying a shovel to extricate the found victim has become a mandatory complement to carrying a transceiver. Most backcountry shovels are designed to fit inside a rucksack or be tied on the outside. While plastic shovels and shovels with T- or L-shaped grips are adequate, aluminum shovels with short or telescoping handles and D-ring grips are best for the backcountry. Folding metal shovels found in army surplus stores are made for digging trenches and are too small for efficient digging but may suffice if nothing else is available. Any shovel is better than a ski tip or hands when moving avalanche debris.

For central avalanche caches (see Appendix A: Avalanche Rescue Caches), the best compromise between effective size and weight is the 12-inch aluminum grain scoop with D-handle. Several of these can be nested in a rucksack or on a pack frame for transport to the accident site. Prolonged digging in hard snow, however, is easier with a steel shovel. The flatter "coal and street cleaner's" model is effective but adds considerable weight. Larger shovels are more effective in soft, light snow, but take too large a bite for easily lifting and throwing in the dense snow characteristic of avalanche debris.

CHAPTER 4
Case Histories

Reading about the mistakes of others is an effective way to learn how to avoid similar errors. That is why the early editions of this handbook concluded with several case histories of avalanche accidents and rescue efforts. They have been removed from subsequent editions because a much larger collection is now available elsewhere. Each decade or so, the U.S. Department of Agriculture Forest Service sponsors the publication of U.S. avalanche case histories in the *Snowy Torrents* series (Gallagher 1967, Williams 1975, Williams and Armstrong 1984, and Logan and Atkins 1996). In addition, Bruce Jamieson and Torsten Geldsetzer's *Avalanche Accidents in Canada* compiles case histories in Canada for the period 1984 to 1996. The reader is strongly urged to consult these publications, study the case histories in detail, and take heed of the many ways in which the mountain traveler can fall victim to sliding snow.

The case histories that follow are of a different kind: they show how experienced people go about evaluating avalanche hazards, and they deal with a wide variety of snow conditions and hazard situations, all of the sort likely to be encountered by winter travelers in the backcountry.

SPRING SKI TOUR TO PARADISE VALLEY, MOUNT RAINIER, APRIL 1976

A ski touring trip was made to Paradise Valley after 2 days of clear weather had followed a spring snowstorm with substantial amounts of new snow at higher elevations on Mount Rainier. Circumstances were ideal for wet-snow avalanches, with strong radiation on south exposures following new snow deposition. By the time Paradise was reached, however, it was obvious that little or no avalanching would occur that day:

1. Freezing level in the atmosphere was reported around 1800 meters (5900 ft), but little melt could be seen above 1500 meters (4900 ft). At the altitude of Paradise, about 1700 meters (5600 ft), there was limited snowmelt even on slopes facing directly south.

2. The only observed avalanching on the second clear day after a spring snowfall was some wet-snow activity on steep, forested slopes below 1200 meters (3900 ft). There was no activity at all on south exposures above 1500 meters (4900 ft), which was unusual for the season and snow conditions.

3. Glacier-fed Tahoma and Kautz Creeks were running clear, indicating that no prolonged melt had been taking place at higher altitudes.

4. New snow persisted on rocks at higher elevations on Mount Rainier in spite of the previous sunny days, again suggesting little or no melt.

5. The snow was very bright in the sunlight, indicating a high reflectivity characteristic of a snow surface with little or no liquid water present.

   During the course of the ski tour to an altitude of about 2500 meters (8200 ft), further observations confirmed the original impression.

6. Surface snow was cold and underlying layers poorly consolidated on shaded and north slopes.

7. By noon, many slopes showed the mirrorlike gleam of firnspiegel, a very thin ice layer produced by a freezing snow surface during sunshine.

8. Local, patchy firnspiegel occurred everywhere underfoot above 1700 meters (5600 ft).

9. There was poor spring skiing (the original purpose of the tour as conceived in Seattle) with no corn snow development at all, even on the second day of hot spring sun.

Diverse observations over several hours had combined to form a picture of cool, dry air, which promoted snow surface evaporation and radiation cooling. This kept the snow surface mostly below freezing in spite of intense spring sunlight on south exposures. The dominant factor preventing normal wet-snow spring avalanches was low atmospheric humidity at these altitudes. This could not easily be measured directly (the nearest Weather Service radiosonde station is at Quillayute, 240 kilometers (150 miles) to the northwest), but it could be clearly inferred from several lines of evidence about snow behavior.

TRAINING COURSE IN THE CARIBOO MOUNTAINS OF BRITISH COLUMBIA, JANUARY 1976

A training course in avalanche safety was planned for helicopter ski guides. In preparation for this course, a prior evaluation of avalanche conditions in the Cariboos was made, then refined after field observations on subsequent days. The preparation began a month in advance by studying weather reports for the Cariboo area.

1. Before the instructor left Seattle, recent storm data affecting the Cariboo area were reviewed. Storms were identified as light and few, indicating a thin snow cover with general kinetic-growth metamorphism to be expected.

2. Valley snow depths observed during the train ride to Valemount varied from 46 centimeters at Blue River to 15 centimeters or less at Valemount. Clear effects were seen of rain on snow followed by 4 to 10 centimeters of new snow, plus general evidence of recent thaw followed by refreezing.

3. During the evening in Valemount, conversations with guides and a helicopter pilot pieced together the picture of a thin snow cover with the last significant snowfall having occurred over a week previously. A subsequent warm period with melt was followed by cold, windy weather. Recent natural avalanches had fallen, mostly from drift areas on high, lee slopes. Current conditions offered good powder skiing mixed with surface crusts and 4 to 7 centimeters of surface hoar on some slopes.

Already a picture of snow and avalanche conditions had emerged without the forecaster ever having set foot on the Cariboo slopes. An estimate of stability was then prepared on evidence to that point.

First Estimate: A shallow, erratically unstable snow cover with mixed layering, moderate to advanced kinetic-growth snow, thaw crust up to 2100 meters (6900 ft), and a tricky and uneven hazard from lee slope drifts above timberline. Extensive hazard could be expected from loading by any appreciable amounts of new snow.

On the next day, avalanche release zones were visited by helicopter, and test pits were dug to collect information about snow cover structure.

4. Snow depths averaged 0.75 to 1 meter with a weak structure involving much kinetic-growth snow plus depth hoar in some places. In areas of deeper drifts, up to 2 meters thick, the snow cover was stronger, but with some kinetic-growth snow at the bottom.
5. Skiing and some shallow, hasty pits confirmed these findings. The snow cover was shallow except in drift areas and generally showed advanced depth hoar development.

At the end of this day of field investigation, a second stability estimate was made, based on direct observation of snow cover structure.

Figure 20. Firnspiegel. ▶

Second Estimate: Little change from first estimate. Snow marginally stable and likely to react to any kind of loading. Some present danger on slopes steeper than 40°, especially in drift areas.

The stability evaluation continued for a second day with a wide-ranging reconnaissance by skiing on slopes of varied altitudes and aspects. Test skiing on small, safe slopes was an important part of this evaluation.

6. Snow cover depth was broadly 0.5 to 0.75 meter, with depth hoar consistently appearing at the bottom.
7. A shallow layer of new snow on top of an old slab avalanche bed surface, the ground, had already converted entirely to very unstable depth hoar.
8. Surface hoar existed on some northeast slopes up to 4 centimeters thick with a thin layer of new snow on top. This would become dangerously unstable with subsequent loading.
9. Numerous very shallow soft slab avalanches had appeared since the previous day among steep rocks and gullies at higher elevations. These had likely been generated by continuing kinetic-growth metamorphism in the recent new snow and were warnings of a developing weak snow surface that would poorly support the next snowfall.

The training group had been skiing very cautiously under these conditions and a consensus had developed among several experienced hands that snow conditions were tricky and could be locally dangerous.

At the end of the second day in the field, a *final* stability evaluation was made.

Final Estimate: Essentially the same as the previous day's estimate. Even a moderate snowfall would create very unstable snow conditions awaiting the triggering action of a skier. A heavy snowfall would actually be safer, once the expected avalanche cycle was over, for it would clean out most steep slopes through natural avalanche releases.

In this case history, the estimate of avalanche danger progressed logically, starting with a broad judgment based on meteorological conditions and proceeding through an examination of snow structure to ski tests of the snow cover's actual mechanical stability. Each successive step added increasingly specific knowledge about snow stability, raising confidence in the accuracy of the original judgment.

AVALANCHES IN BANFF NATIONAL PARK, MARCH 1977

In this example, forecasters were able to predict a very dangerous condition following a seemingly harmless snowstorm because they had paid close attention to the evolution of snow cover structure throughout the winter of 1976–77, one of unusually light snowfalls in the Canadian Rockies.

1. December brought very light snowfalls, yielding a very shallow snow cover with extensive kinetic-growth metamorphism.
2. The same conditions persisted into January. Depth

hoar formation was extensive. Widespread avalanching following any heavy snowfall was already being predicted.

3. The same weather pattern continued into February. Toward the middle of the month an episode of surface hoar formation was widely observed in the Canadian Rockies. This layer of highly unstable crystals was subsequently buried by light snowfalls.

4. The light winter continued on into March, with some improvements in snow quantities. Skiers were frequently involved in avalanche accidents, with thirteen separate incidents having occurred around the Sunshine ski area by late March. New avalanches were forming with snowfalls of as little as 2 to 5 centimeters.

5. There were seven avalanche fatalities after mid-March in the Canadian Rockies and adjacent ranges. The February surface hoar layer appeared to have been the major cause of these accidents.

6. A storm arrived in the Banff–Sunshine area early on March 26. By the morning of the 27th, 25 centimeters of snow had fallen, and the wind was averaging 4.5 m/s. The Banff Warden staff issued a public warning of *extreme* avalanche hazard, labeling some slopes as "suicidal."

7. The storm continued until evening of the 27th. A major avalanche cycle developed during the afternoon, with many large, natural releases between 2:00 and 3:00 p.m. Many skiers in the Banff–Sunshine area failed to heed the warnings. Nine persons were caught in avalanches, four were injured, and one died.

By usual mountain weather standards, this late-March storm was almost trivial, with 33 centimeters total snowfall spread out over a 40-hour period. Many such storms occur in most areas each year without causing such extensive avalanching, but in this case an extremely unstable structure in the shallow snow cover was ready to react to even this modest loading. By following the winter-long evolution of the snow cover and noting the accumulating evidence from earlier avalanches, forecasters were able to anticipate very accurately what was going to happen. This was a situation where, clearly, "the forecast began with the first snowfall of winter."

SIX EVENTS IN THE CASCADE MOUNTAINS

The following is a compilation of snow conditions that led up to six avalanche accidents or events at different times. In this instance the source is not an experienced avalanche hand but the Seattle newspapers, which often report avalanche accidents on the front page and with prominent headlines. An instructive common theme runs through these stories, connected by the incidental mention of snow and weather.

1. "[M]ore than a foot [30 cm] of new, wet snow fell yesterday. The National Weather Service had a travelers' warning out with extreme avalanche danger in the Cascades. They forecast heavy snow through today. . . ."

2. "Numerous slides were reported in the park as warm, rainy weather hit the area yesterday . . . gale winds,

rain, sleet and snow raked the mountain yesterday. . . . "

3. "Eleven inches [28 cm] of snow fell at the pass overnight. . . . The Forest Service warned that an extreme avalanche hazard existed in the mountains. . . . The slides were caused by a sudden warming that raised the freezing level to about 4500 ft [1400 m]."

4. " 'Avalanche warnings were ignored,' he said. 'We just didn't check the conditions' . . . conditions that turned worse from morning rain and midday sun on the wet, heavy snow."

5. "The Forest Service had posted a high avalanche hazard for the Cascade Mountains over the weekend because of heavy snowfall. Eighteen inches [46 cm] of new snow fell in the 3 days before the avalanche."

6. Report of an August mountaineering accident: "There was a high-pressure ridge growing and a declining chance of rain. We decided it looked feasible. . . ." [Survivor] "But we've had 18 inches [46 cm] of fresh snow in the area in the past week, and there was a sheet avalanche up there that just gave way." [Investigator]

Many avalanches in the Cascades are precipitated by obvious meteorological causes, most prominently a heavy fall of new snow or a sudden rain or thaw. A combination of new snow followed immediately by thaw or rain is even more effective. Weather forecasts and warning bulletins usually give from 12 to 36 hours' notice of such events. By following weather evolution a day or two prior to a trip, or at least checking on hazard warnings the day of departure, winter recreationists can be apprised of dangerous conditions. If there is an avalanche information service in the area, it should be consulted. Close attention in the field can also help one recognize the rapid onset of danger. A drastic increase in snowfall, a sudden temperature rise, or rain starting to fall on cold snow can very quickly alter snow stability for the worse.

A WEEK OF SKI TOURING ON THE RUTH GLACIER (MOUNT McKINLEY), APRIL 1983

The occasion was a planned week of ski touring among the peaks surrounding the Ruth Glacier. This is a remote area, where no weather or avalanche reports are available and only the most general weather patterns can be deduced. Close attention has to be paid to whatever field evidence of snow stability can be obtained as the trip evolves.

1. Winter had lingered late in the Alaska Range, and the usual April periods of fair weather had not yet appeared. Recent new snow and cold conditions were to be expected.

2. On the ski plane flight from Talkeetna a careful observation of how the snow lay on the mountains showed no evidence of recent, major avalanches except for isolated glacier icefalls. Fresh sluffs and small avalanches were scattered on very steep slopes. The snow-covered glacier surfaces showed evidence of only light wind drifting, but there was substantial cornice formation on the ridges.

3. An initial snow structure check was made while setting up camp on the glacier. A quick pit about 1.5 meters deep showed cold, unconsolidated snow in the top layers with solid, well-bonded older snow at depth. A quick shovel test did not reveal any seriously weak shear planes.
4. A short ski tour to adjacent slopes identified weak snow layers to a depth of 46 to 60 centimeters, with some light surface slabbing on windward slopes.

First Estimate: Plenty of unsettled, recent new snow, with likelihood of soft slab development higher on the ridges. Degree of instability still unknown. Be very cautious!

Intermittent snow fell over the next 3 days, at times accompanied by strong winds and near-blizzard conditions. About 0.5 meter of new snow accumulated during this period. There was no safe, reliable place to find a test slope in these poor weather conditions. Snow stability was expected to get worse with the snowfalls and wind drifting, so great caution was required. Some actual avalanches needed to be observed to confirm this judgment.

5. A slope near camp avalanched, possibly triggered by a mild earthquake. The dust cloud and light wind blast reached the campsite.
6. Clearing weather revealed that several soft slab avalanches had run from the higher ridge crests. An actual fall was witnessed.

◀ *Figure 21. Skiing on the Ruth Glacier.*

7. A climbing party arrived in the area after an attempt on a nearby peak. They reported that while high in a couloir they encountered difficult going in deep, soft snow over a wind crust. On their descent they narrowly escaped being caught when this entire couloir avalanched.

Final Estimate: A marginal avalanche situation had rapidly evolved to a dangerous one with additional snowfalls. The meteorological evidence had pointed to this and was confirmed by observed avalanche falls. This was no time to be playing around on the steep slopes and ridges. Ski touring would be confined to gentle glacier slopes.

In a situation like this the avalanche danger could not be assessed beforehand, but had to be judged by a continuous appraisal of current conditions as the trip progressed. It is essential to be alert to different lines of evidence and to be very cautious until clear information turns up concerning what the snow stability is really like.

SUMMARY

These case histories have a common theme: avalanche forecasting as an ongoing process. The time spans involved are diverse, ranging from hours through a few days to an entire winter. In each case, evidence about snow stability is collected early, then continually supplemented with evidence from many additional sources. Progressive estimates of avalanche danger are made, each revising and improving on the previous one. The meteorological evidence (Class III) is often the starting point, providing a general appraisal of snow conditions. As the process evolves, more and more Class II and Class I evidence is sought to support increasingly specific estimates of avalanche danger. Observations or reports of actual avalanche occurrences provide solid confirmation about decreasing snow stability. The final decisions are based on a chain of evidence that progressively clarifies the initial uncertainties.

There is no one formula that will identify avalanche danger, no magic box that will flash a warning light when the snow is unstable. Reaching a clear evaluation requires constant attention and analysis. The practitioners in these examples were all doing what had become a habit: *They were always thinking about snow conditions.* It's a habit worth adopting, for survival often depends on it.

Appendix A
Avalanche Rescue Caches

Careful advance planning and preparation are essential to orderly and effective rescue. Avalanche rescue caches equipped with necessary supplies should be placed at readily accessible points in areas of high avalanche hazard. All caches should contain as a minimum for each departing group of rescuers:

- Electronic transceivers
- Collapsible avalanche probes
- Climbing skins
- Climbing rope
- Headlamps
- Portable two-way radio

CACHES FOR STAGES OF RESCUE

The following specialized equipment is required during the main stages of rescue:

STAGE ONE—LOCATION AND RECOVERY OF THE VICTIM

- Avalanche probes (thin-walled steel tubing is by far the best)
- First-aid kit
- Resuscitator
- Filament tape and nylon cord

- Shovel pack containing D-handle aluminum shovels
- Wands or flags
- Ball of cord or heavy string
- Flares
- Area map and compass

STAGE TWO—FIRST AID AND TRANSPORT OF THE VICTIM

- Resuscitator oxygen
- First-aid kit
- Physician's medical kit
- Sectional toboggans
- Winter sleeping bags
- First-aid tent
- Portable stove

STAGE THREE—LOGISTICAL SUPPORT FOR PROLONGED RESCUES

- Avalanche probes
- Portable stoves
- Flares
- Portable floodlights
- Blankets
- Food
- Sleeping bags
- Tent
- Extra clothing

These suggestions are the bare minimum. Additional equipment, such as an electronic megaphone, is also useful.

CENTRALLY LOCATED CACHES IN AVALANCHE TERRAIN

The following is minimum equipment that should be available at all times in a central location at ski and climbing areas in avalanche terrain:

- 12 probes (sectional preferred; otherwise, metal rods or tubes 10 mm in diameter, minimum 3–4 meters long; thin-walled steel or carbon-fiber tubing is recommended)
- 12 snow shovels
- 12 electric headlamps; carton of spare batteries
- 50-meter climbing rope
- First-aid kit (standard ski patrolman's kit is satisfactory)
- Toboggan with blankets (collapsible toboggan light enough to be backpacked is preferred)

The following additional equipment is recommended:

- Emergency rations
- Chemical hot pads for toboggan
- Gasoline stoves
- Camp cook kit
- Mountain tent
- Climbers
- Gasoline lanterns
- Portable two-way radio (USFS, ski patrol, etc.)

Appendix B
Avalanche Accident and Rescue Report

The following report outline is designed to furnish legal and statistical information to civil authorities. It is not suitable for medical personnel reporting details of the victim's condition. Complete the report and send a copy to the nearest regional avalanche center (see list of centers in Appendix C).

1. Date, time, and location of accident
2. Names of victims and other members of party
   - Describe their mountain and avalanche experience
   - State their current activity
   - List number caught in avalanche
   - List number partially buried
   - List number completely buried with the depth and duration of burial
   - List number injured or dead
3. If vehicles involved, describe the number that were trapped, completely buried, partially buried, or damaged, and their type.
4. Summary of events leading to accident: departure point, route, and destination or objective. Include where the victim(s) were relative to the starting zone when the avalanche struck.
5. Description of the avalanche:
   - Aspect
   - Elevation

- Angle of slope
- Whether loose or slab
- Whether wet or dry
- If slab, describe its thickness and sliding layer if known

6. Eyewitness account of accident, if available; otherwise, observer's deductions based on tracks and any other evidence; important points (location of skier in relation to release point of slide); assessment of how slide was released.

7. Summary of rescue operations (times and names are important):
   - Time of accident
   - Time accident reported and by whom
   - Time first party dispatched and name of leader
   - Number in party
   - Time of first party's arrival at accident site
   - Procedure at site
   - Time victim is found
   - Location of victim at time of discovery
   - Injuries sustained by victim
   - Cause of death, or other outcome
   - Time operation concluded

8. Weather and avalanche background: wind, temperature, and snow data; avalanche restrictions in force, if any; type of slide and extent.

9. Terrain data, including maps and diagrams

10. Recommendations and conclusions

Appendix C
Avalanche Information Bulletins

Before embarking on a trip to the mountains, especially if it is your first trip of the season, obtain an avalanche information bulletin. These can be found at some park entrances or forest information stations or by calling or visiting the website of your nearest avalanche information center. Each center provides the most current information on mountain weather and avalanche hazard.

AVALANCHE INFORMATION CENTERS

Current telephone numbers can be found at most websites.
>   North America: *www.avalanche.org*
>   Europe: *www.lawinen.org*
>   New Zealand: *www.avalanche.net.nz*

AVALANCHE DANGER SCALE

Most avalanche information bulletins begin with a general description of the regional danger level, then offer specific clues about how to recognize and/or negotiate the danger. Remember, distinctions given in regional reports between geographic areas, elevations, slope aspect, and slope angle are approximate. Local snow cover conditions vary widely. Therefore, this basic information is designed only to give you a head start on your own safety evaluation.

UNITED STATES AVALANCHE DANGER SCALE (1997)

Danger Level	Why	Where	What to do
LOW (green)	Natural avalanches unlikely. Human-triggered avalanches **unlikely.**	Generally stable snow. Isolated areas of instability.	Travel is generally safe. Normal caution advised.
MODERATE (yellow)	Natural avalanches unlikely. Human-triggered avalanches **possible.**	Unstable slabs possible on steep terrain.	Use caution in steeper terrain on certain aspects.
CONSIDERABLE (orange)	Natural avalanches possible. Human-triggered avalanche **probable.**	Unstable slabs probable on steep terrain.	Be increasingly cautious in steeper terrain.
HIGH (red)	Natural and human-triggered avalanches **likely.**	Unstable slabs likely on a variety of aspects and slope angles.	Travel in avalanche terrain is not recommended. Safest travel on windward ridges of lower-angle slopes without steeper terrain above.
EXTREME (red with black border)	Widespread natural or human-triggered avalanches **certain.**	Extremely unstable slabs certain on most aspects and slope angles. Large destructive avalanches possible.	Travel in avalanche terrain should be avoided and travel confined to low-angle terrain well away from avalanche path runouts.

OTHER SOURCES OF AVALANCHE INFORMATION

American Avalanche Association:
www.americanavalancheassociation.org

Canadian Avalanche Association: *www.avalanche.ca*

Swiss Federal Institute for Snow and Avalanche
Research: *www.slf.ch*

USDA Forest Service, National Avalanche Center:
www.fsavalanche.org

Short Bibliography of Avalanche Literature

Avalanche Accidents in Canada, by Bruce Jamieson and Torsten Geldsetzer. Revelstoke, B.C.: Canadian Avalanche Association, 1996.

Avalanche Atlas, by International Commission on Snow and Ice of the International Association of Hydrologic Sciences. Paris: UNESCO, 1981. Out of print but may be found in libraries.

Avalanche Awareness: A Practical Guide to Safe Travel in Avalanche Terrain, by John Moynier. Evergreen, Colo.: Chockstone Press, 1993.

The Avalanche Book, Revised and Updated, by Betsy Armstrong and Knox Williams. Golden, Colo.: Fulcrum, 1992. Out of print but may be found in libraries.

The Avalanche Handbook, by David McClung and Peter Schaerer. Seattle: The Mountaineers Books, 2000.

The Avalanche Hunters, by Montgomery M. Atwater. Philadelphia: McCrae Smith Company, 1968. Out of print but may be found in libraries.

The Avalanche Review, a serial publication of the American Avalanche Association, P.O. Box 2831, Pagosa Springs, CO 81147. Visit *www.americanavalancheassociation.org.*

Avalanche Safety for Skiers and Climbers, 2nd Edition, by Tony Daffern. Seattle: The Mountaineers Books, 2000.

"Avalanches," by Malcolm Mellor, in *Cold Regions Science and Engineering,* Part III, Section A3. Hanover, N.H.: U.S. Army CRREL, May 1968. Out of print but may be found in libraries.

Avalanches and Snow Safety, by Colin Fraser. New York: Charles Scribner's Sons, 1978. Out of print but may be found in libraries.

Backcountry Avalanche Awareness, 7th Edition, by Bruce Jamieson. Revelstoke, B.C.: Canadian Avalanche Association, 2000.

A Chance in a Million? Scottish Avalanches, by Bob Barton and Blyth Wright. Leicester, England: Scottish Mountaineering Club and Trust, 2000.

Field Guide to Snow Crystals, by Edward R. LaChapelle. Cambridge, England: International Glaciological Society, 2001.

Free Riding in Avalanche Terrain: A Snowboarder's Handbook, by Bruce Jamieson and Torsten Geldsetzer. Revelstoke, B.C.: Canadian Avalanche Association, 1999.

International Classification for Seasonal Snow on the Ground, by S. Colbeck, E. Akitaya, R. Armstrong, H. Gubler, J. Lafeuill, K. Lied, D. McClung, and E. Morris, International Commission of Snow and Ice. Boulder, Colo.: World Data Center A for Glaciology, 1990.

Mountaineering: The Freedom of the Hills, 7th Edition, edited by Steven M. Cox and Kris Fulsaas. Seattle: The Mountaineers Books, 2003.

Secrets of the Snow: Visual Clues to Avalanches and Ski Conditions, by Edward R. LaChapelle. Seattle: University of Washington Press, 2001.

Sledding in Avalanche Terrain, by Bruce Jamieson and Darcy Svederus. Revelstoke, B.C.: Canadian Avalanche Association, 1998.

Snow Sense: A Guide to Evaluating Snow Avalanche Hazard, 4th Edition, by Jill Fredston and Doug Fester. Anchorage: Alaska Mountain Safety Center, Inc., 1994.

Snow Structures and Ski Fields, by Gerald Seligman. Cambridge, England: International Glaciological Society, 1980. Scarce and hard to find, but beautifully illustrated and a basic text in the field. Photo-offset editions in limited quantities are sometimes available through the International Glaciological Society.

The Snowy Torrents: Avalanche Accidents in the United States, 1910–66, by Dale Gallagher. Alta, Utah: U.S. Forest Service, Alta Avalanche Study Center, 1967.

The Snowy Torrents: Avalanche Accidents in the United States, 1967–71, by Knox Williams. USDA Forest Service General Technical Report RM-8, 1975. Second edition published by Teton Bookshop Publishing Company, Jackson Hole, Wyo., 1981.

The Snowy Torrents: Avalanche Accidents in the United States, 1972–79, by Knox Williams and Betsy Armstrong. Jackson Hole, Wyo.: Teton Bookshop Publishing Company, 1984.

The Snowy Torrents: Avalanche Accidents in the United States, 1980–86, by Nick Logan and Dale Atkins. Denver, Colo.: Colorado Geological Survey, 1996.

The first three volumes of this publication are out of print but may be obtained in libraries. The fourth volume may be ordered from the Colorado Avalanche Information Center, *www.caic.state.co.us.*

Staying Alive in Avalanche Terrain, by Bruce Tremper. Seattle: The Mountaineers Books, 2001.

Index

A

age hardening, 28
air blast. *See* wind blast
air temperature, 58–59
avalanche(s)
  beacon. *See* transceivers
  danger scale, 133–134
  definition, 8
  factors contributing to, 44–72
  formation of, 45–46, 59–60
  return interval, 10
  summer dangers of, 70–72
  track. *See* avalanche path
avalanche cord. *See* rescue, cord
avalanche beacon. *See* transceivers
avalanche danger scale, 133–134
avalanche forecasting, 61–72, 112–127
  analyzing evidence, 61–72
  basic rules, 64–65
  guidelines, 65–70
  information centers, 133–135
  nature of, 61–62
  problems, 62–63
avalanche fractures
  as evidence of instability, 45–56
  bed surface, 14, 36
  crown, 13–14
  external triggers, 14, 34, 37–41
  flank, 13–14
  glide cracks, 18
  gliding surface, 12
  internal triggers, 33–34, 41
  stauchwall, 13–14
avalanche path
  channeled, 12
  definition, 10
  deposition zone. *See* avalanche
     path, runout zone
  release zone, 9, 10, 41
  runout zone, 9,10
  starting zone. *See* avalanche
     path, release zone
  track, 9, 10, 41
  unconfined, 12
avalanche probe. *See* rescue, probe
avalanche terrain
  definition, 40–43
  rules for travel in, 43, 73–81
avalanche types
  climax, 12
  dry, 14
  full-depth, 12
  hard, 14, 66–68
  loose-snow, 12, 31–32
  point-release. *See* avalanche
     types, loose-snow
  powder, 16, 17
  slab, 12, 14, 32–36, 38, 65–70
  sluff, 10–12, 66
  slush flow, 17
  soft, 14, 38, 65–66
  transavalanche, 18
  wet, 14, 32, 37–38, 64, 68–70,
    114

B

beacon. *See* transceivers
bed surface. *See* avalanche
  fractures, bed surface
burial, 81–83, 99–101

C

caches. *See* rescue, caches
case histories, 112–127

cornice, 37, 58, 75, 123
creep. See snow mechanics, creep
crusts. See snow layer(s), crusts
crystals. See snow crystals

D

danger. See avalanche danger scale
density. See snow density
deposition zone. See avalanche
  path, runout zone
depth hoar. See snow crystals,
  depth hoar
dogs. See rescue, dogs
dust cloud, 17

F

firnspiegel, 114, 117
flank. See avalanche fractures,
  flank
forecasting. See avalanche
  forecasting
fracture. See avalanche fractures
freezing level, 113

G

glide. See snow mechanics, glide
glide cracks. See avalanche
  fractures, glide cracks
graupel, 20, 21

H

hoarfrost. See snow crystals,
  surface hoar

I

ice avalanches, 72, 123

L

loose-snow avalanches. See
  avalanche types, loose-snow

lubricating layer. See snow layer(s),
  weak layer

M

metamorphism. See snow
  metamorphism

P

point release. See avalanche types,
  loose-snow
precipitation intensity, 56–57,
  65–66
probes. See rescue, probes

R

rain, 17, 31, 59, 68–69, 70, 115, 123
release zone. See avalanche path,
  release zone
rescue
  beacon. See transceivers
  by survivors, 81–92
  by organized teams, 93–102
  caches, 111, 128–130
  cord, 105–106
  dogs, 103–105
  equipment, 74, 86, 88–89, 95–97,
    105–111
  first aid, 98–101
  multiple burials, 92
  precautions, 97–98
  probes, 74, 86, 91, 92, 94–98,
    102, 106–107, 128, 130
  reporting, 131–132
return interval. See avalanche(s),
  return interval
rime. See snow crystal(s), rime
risks, 73–81
route finding. See avalanche terrain
runout zone. See avalanche path,
  runout zone

rutschblock test. *See* snow stability, evaluation

S

settlement. *See* snow mechanics, settlement

slab. *See* avalanche types, slab

slab layer(s). *See* snow layer(s)

shovels, 74, 110, 111

shovel test. *See* snow stability, evaluation

slope angle, 17, 40, 42, 75

slope settlement. *See* snow mechanics, settlement

sluffs. *See* avalanche types, sluff

slush flow. *See* avalanche types, slush flow

snow
  pillow, 36
  properties, 28–31
  rules about, 64

snow cover
  defined, 10
  formation of, 21–28
  stability. *See* snow stability

snow crystals
  columns, 19–20
  corn snow, 114
  cups. *See* depth hoar
  dendrites, 19–20, 57
  depth hoar, 25, 38, 48, 54, 61, 64, 67, 69, 119
  formation of, 19–28
  graupel, 20–21, 36, 53, 56
  hoarfrost. *See* snow crystals, surface hoar
  needles, 19–20, 57
  plates, 19–20, 57
  rime, 19–21, 57
  sheaths, 19

stellars. *See* snow crystals, dendrites

sugar snow. *See* snow crystals, depth hoar

surface hoar, 20–21, 36, 53, 67

snow density 57, 66

snow depth, 52–53, 57, 104, 115–118

snow layer(s)
  bed layer, 12, 14, 36, 52–54
  configuration, 53–54
  crusts, 28, 33, 36, 49, 52, 53, 70, 116
  definition, 21, 35–36, 53
  lubricating layer. *See* snow layer(s), weak layer
  slab layer(s), 12, 21–22, 35–37, 41, 53–54
  variability, 38–39
  weak layer, 14, 27, 38, 53–54

snow mechanics
  collapse test. *See* snow stability, evaluation
  compression test. *See* snow stability, evaluation
  creep, 18, 28
  glide, 18, 28
  properties, 28, 54–55
  rutschblock test. *See* snow stability, evaluation
  settlement, 17–18, 46
  shovel test. *See* snow stability, evaluation
  stuff-block test. *See* snow stability, evaluation
  tilt test. *See* snow stability, evaluation

snow metamorphism
  constructive. *See* snow metamorphism, kinetic-growth

definition, 21–28
destructive. *See* snow metamorphism, equilibrium
ET. *See* snow metamorphism, equilibrium
equilibrium, 22–25, 54, 64
kinetic-growth, 24–27, 33, 37, 38, 54, 116, 118, 119
radius-dependent recrystallization. *See* snow metamorphism, equilibrium
TG. *See* snow metamorphism, kinetic-growth
wet, 26–28
snow stability
evaluation, 46–52, 53, 62–65
evidence of, 44–59
snow crystals and, 53–54
weather and, 56–59, 113
snow temperature, 25, 28, 29–31, 55–56, 58, 65, 75
thermal properties, 29–31, 55–56, 64
snowfall, 56–59
intensity, 56, 119, 121, 123
snowpack. *See* snow cover
snowslide. *See* avalanche(s)
stability. *See* snow stability
starting zone. *See* avalanche path, release zone
stauchwall. *See* avalanche fractures, stauchwall
stuff-block test. *See* snow stability, evaluation
sugar snow. *See* snow crystals, depth hoar
summer snow. *See* avalanche(s), summer dangers of

surface hoar. *See* snow crystals, surface hoar

T
terrain. *See* avalanche terrain
test skiing, 76–77
track. *See* avalanche path
transceivers
equipment, 74, 88–89, 91–92, 108–111, 128
multiple burials, 92
search patterns, 87–92
use of, 74, 78, 85, 109–110
transavalanche. *See* avalanche types, transavalanche

V
victims
care of, 87, 99–101
if caught, 79–81
rescue of, 81–92
survival chances of, 81–84
transport of, 98–101

W
weak layer. *See* snow layer(s), weak layer
weather, 56–59, 113
weathering, 64
wet snow, 26–28, 31, 32, 33, 53, 68–70
wind blast, 17, 125
wind drifted snow, 33, 53, 57–58, 59, 67, 115, 116, 125
wet snow metamorphism. *See* snow metamorphism, wet
wet-snow avalanche. *See* avalanche types, wet

About the Authors

Sue A. Ferguson, after receiving her Ph.D. in geophysics and atmospheric sciences under Ed's tutelage from the University of Washington, directed the Utah Avalanche Center and was lead avalanche and mountain weather forecaster at the Alaska Avalanche Center and the Northwest Weather and Avalanche Center. She founded *The Avalanche Review* and co-founded the American Avalanche Association. She is an active skier and glacier explorer. Her books include *Glaciers of North America: A Field Guide,* Fulcrum Publishing, 1992, and the "Cycle of Snow" chapter in *Mountaineering: The Freedom of the Hills,* 7th edition, The Mountaineers Books, 2003.

Edward (Ed) R. LaChapelle, formerly head of the U.S. Forest Service Avalanche Center in Alta, Utah, and professor emeritus of geophysics and atmospheric sciences at the University of Washington, is one of the foremost American authorities on avalanches. He is also an active skier and mountaineer with expedition experience ranging from Greenland to Alaska. His most recent books include *Secrets of the Snow: Visual Clues to Avalanches and Ski Conditions,* University of Washington Press, 2001; and a reprint of *Field Guide to Snow Crystals* from the International Glaciological Society, 2001.

THE MOUNTAINEERS, founded in 1906, is a nonprofit outdoor activity and conservation club with seven branches, whose mission is "to explore, study, preserve, and enjoy the natural beauty of the outdoors . . . . " The club sponsors many classes and year-round outdoor activities in the Pacific Northwest, and supports environmental causes through educational activities, sponsoring legislation, and presenting educational programs. The Mountaineers Books supports the club's mission by publishing travel and natural history guides, instructional texts, and works on conservation and history.

Send or call for our catalog of more than 500 outdoor titles:

The Mountaineers Books
1001 SW Klickitat Way, Suite 201
Seattle, WA 98134
800-553-4453
mbooks@mountaineersbooks.org
www.mountaineersbooks.org

Leave No Trace strives to educate visitors about the nature of their recreational impacts, as well as offer techniques to prevent and minimize such impacts. Leave No Trace is best understood as an educational and ethical program, not as a set of rules and regulations.

For more information, visit *www.LNT.org,* or call 800-332-4100.